D1391820

TRAINING FROM THE GROUND

A Special Approach

TRAINING FROM THE GROUND

A Special Approach

The Marquis MacSwiney
of Mashanaglass

Foreword by Sylvia Stanier LVO

J.A. ALLEN
London

First published in Great Britain by
J. A. Allen & Co Ltd
1 Lower Grosvenor Place
London SW1W 0EL
1987

Reprinted 1991
Reprinted 1995

British Library Cataloguing in Publication Data

MacSwiney of Mashanaglass, *Marquis*
    Training from the ground: a special approach.
    1. Horses——Training
    I. Title
    636.1′083   SF287

    ISBN 0–85131–429–5

Line illustrations by Elaine How

Phototypeset in 12 on 13 point Bembo by
Input Typesetting Ltd, London
Printed and bound by Butler & Tanner,
Frome, Somerset

To

Patrick

*Only son, friend, companion, dog-
and horse-lover, who did so much
work on this book.*

(b. 24.7.1956 – d. 4.2.1985)

Contents

CONTENTS

Foreword and Appreciation

by Sylvia Stanier LVO

THE MARQUIS MACSWINEY OF MASHANAGLASS (1916–1986)

In the early 1950s, when I lived in Dublin, I met a person who I now know was Owen MacSwiney. He was a most sophisticated and cultured man and he left me with an impression of being highly intelligent, kindly and artistic.

Owen MacSwiney was born in Dublin in 1916. He was fascinated by horses all his life although for many years this interest was interrupted by business commitments. He went to University College, Dublin, studied law at King's Inn and was called to the bar. He later took up a career in international fashion and design, eventually making his home in Westphalia, Germany. A man of many talents Owen MacSwiney was also a renowned artist and sculptor.

When Owen was a small boy, his paternal grandmother, Countess Konorska, introduced him to horses. She was a friend and pupil of James Fillis. Owen's grandfather had an estate at St Germain-en-Laye, outside Paris, with its own indoor riding arena. His grandmother was also a champion pistol shot and dressage rider in her time; a member of the exclusive L'Etrier Club, she was entitled to wear the Tricorne hat – a lady of some talent. Owen's mother was an excellent rider too, and it was through his mother's sister, who lived in Germany, that he received his first proper tuition – from her coachman. He appears to have been an excellent teacher, passing on much practical knowledge. This, together with his inherited talent, led Owen to become a master, and his expertise has now been written down so clearly in this book.

FOREWORD

Owen MacSwiney was the supreme amateur who had the time and the inclination to prove and research the science and the application of both animal and bird behaviour. He had the freedom to go and see for himself without the restrictions of a professional. He conducted experiments on the behaviour of mute swans, pheasants, snow geese and dogs. His book on mute swans, *Six Came Flying*, was published in several languages. For the last twelve years of his life he devoted his time to experimenting with horses, with the aid of his son Patrick to whom this book is dedicated. The horses used in the experiments were mostly spoiled Westphalians – when I say 'spoiled' I mean horses with a problem, either frightened or in some way unwilling to do what man expected of them. Owen MacSwiney found that by using certain techniques from the ground, such as long reining, working in-hand, and especially using the 'Touch Points' – whereby, for example, the horse's sensory nerve on its ribs is touched causing the animal to move on quite quietly – stress was reduced and the animal induced to work calmly.

We must be grateful to him for his tenacity in discovering things which others may not have had the inclination to pursue. It is sad he did not live to see this book produced in print but we can be glad that he managed to write it all down in time. We must thank him for giving us an insight into what can be achieved with patience and thought.

SYLVIA STANIER LVO
December, 1986

Preface

This book is mainly concerned with teaching young horses in-hand, getting them ready for the day that they will come under saddle and rider. It is also dedicated to the reschooling of horses which have been mishandled and spoiled, or which have never properly learned their business. No-one can deny that the horse we have in our stable is the horse we make. No more, no less. The basic training which I advocate is by far the most effective if one starts the horse very young. But if this is not possible, it is no less effective in working with older horses.

There are experts who do not agree with work in-hand. They say one can teach a horse everything from the saddle. I do not believe that they are totally wrong, but I like to get a horse into my hands before it comes under the saddle and to make it up to the moment that it is first backed and ridden.

It is possible, as well as relatively simple, to develop the kind of horse one would best like to have. Horses, if not spoiled or frightened, are willing, alert, eager to learn and therefore easy to teach, providing you are prepared to take care. Horses which have had a bad experience may best be reschooled in-hand by teaching them new ways and new relationships. In-hand work is ideal for steadying the nerves of anxious animals. I hope that the text of the book will illustrate this as well as giving the reasons why it is so.

All horses, because of their size and strength, are potentially dangerous animals when they get out of control and a really disobedient horse that has learned to have its way is not to be trifled with. Handling makes the horse a safe member of society, in which it has its own special place.

The education and training of horses must be progressive, planned step by step and inseparable from daily handling.

For this reason, it is a mistake, and a very amateur one, to demand too much at any time, or not to repeat lessons even when one believes that the horse is past all training.

In order to achieve one's ends with greater ease, it is in the interest of the horse and trainer, to teach the pupil a vocabulary of human words linked with certain actions. It depends upon the individual intelligence of the animal how quickly it learns such action-linked words. Although teaching an often highly intelligent creature, it is vital to remember that it does not understand concepts too readily. Its innocent mind is only capable of limited conceptual thought. Before teaching, the trainer must therefore decide which words he considers to be the most important and then what actions he wishes to link them to. In practice, both action and word will be taught at the same time.

I have attempted to suggest a logical sequence of teaching in-hand by establishing priorities from my personal experiments and practice.

One of the first things that will strike the attentive reader and possibly even irritate him, will be the frequent use of the adjective *gentle*. The repeated use is deliberate. It is intended to remind the reader that everything in the text has to do with patience and gentleness. The tone of voice used, the touch of the fingers, the general pattern of the approach, must always be quiet, confident and gentle. This underlying gentleness is at the root of everything that we intend to do or teach.

To give an example; there is no need to use a harsh voice or to give a horse a rough push in the ribs when you want it to move aside in its box. A softly spoken 'over' and, if need be, a feather-light touch on the flank with the fingertips will do the job better. The horse will become neither frightened nor resentful if we handle it in this way.

But the employment of the gentle touch and the quiet voice does not mean that you should be silly and sentimental. The trainer is going to have to be authoritarian at times, very much the boss and always the leader in every good and bad situation that may arise. If everything does not run quite to your liking, if you meet with obstinacy or unwillingness, you are going to make sure that you win out in the end. And this will be achieved without the demeaning use of force, or the loud voice or recourse to the whip. The good trainer knows that these things can have only an adverse effect, because he has taken the trouble to understand something about the nature of horses generally.

The good trainer, professional or amateur, will neither treat his horse as inferior nor superior to himself, but rather with respect for what it is, a horse.

Acknowledgements

No book of this nature can be written and brought to a conclusion without the interest and support of others who help, either directly or by assent.

My special thanks are due to publishers who have given me permission to quote verbatim from those who have defined a point better than I could do so myself, or whose material would have to be re-written in order to circumvent the laws of copyright. I would therefore like to thank Mr Joseph Allen of J. A. Allen and Co., London, for his permission to use the late Henry Wynmalen's definition of good hands (*Equitation*, p. 35) and the definition of equine intelligence (p. 42 of the same). His permission was also given to quote from R. S. Summerhays' book *The Problem Horse*, p. 81, and from Neil Dougall's *Stallions*, p. 27, as well as from the preface of Miss Diana Tuke's book, *Horse by Horse*. I also owe a debt of thanks to Mr Michael Harris, Editor of *Pacemaker International*, for allowing me to quote extensively from an article by Mr Michael Clower concerning the death of the National Hunt gelding Golden Cygnet. Thanks to the Deutsche Verlags-Anstalt GmbH, Stuttgart, for permission to quote from the translation into German, from the book by the late Lord Mottistone (General Jack Seely) *Mein Pferd Warrior* (*My Horse Warrior*), as well as the present Lord Mottistone for his help. The works quoted above appear in the chapter by chapter references as well as in the bibliography.

My sincerest thanks are due to my prepublication readers, for their advice and criticism: Herr 'Enno' Albert of the Düsseldorfer Reit- und Rennverein and Frau Angelika von Wedel for reading and encouraging. Dr Janet Kear of the Wildfowl Trust for reading two chapters, well off her normal subject, but for giving a valuable 'outsider's' view, especially on Chapter 6, with which she does not agree. It is difficult to imagine more advice, help and encouragement than has been given me by Colonel William Hurrell of the 17th/ 21st Lancers, stationed at Münster.

I must also thank my son, Patrick, for typing the manuscript and for his humour, forbearance and laughter during the difficult task of working with his father. Thanks too, to my daughter, Baroness Walburga von Aretin, on whose estate my horses have been kept and who has always co-operated. A word of thanks to my wife, who has so often proved herself to be a reliable commentator on my work.

Lastly, my thanks go to the many owners and the many horses involved in experiments of one kind or another, including the main 'guinea pigs', my own mare Tirade and the newcomer, the pony Leila, belonging to my granddaughter and presently learning the business.

PART ONE

CHAPTER I

The Horse: The Animal

IT GOES WITHOUT SAYING that the attitudes of domestic horses differ from those of wild or primitive members of their kind. This is not only due to their long lines of traditional domesticity, but also to the outcome of selective breeding as well as, to a very great extent, the manner of keeping, handling and training of the individual.

Notwithstanding this, all domestic horses retain characteristics of their origin, which allow us to anticipate their reflexes and reactions. It is these common characteristics that make a horse essentially a horse. Behavioural patterns, described by Vavra[1] and Zeeb[2] in relation to wild herds, may also be observed in small groupings of domestic horses, down to as low a number as two – but with subtle differences – because it is part of the horse's nature to set up a social order under any prevailing conditions. Vavra, citing Klingel, says there are important differences in equine social structures from race to race, so that it is logical to regard domestic horses as a separate entity. Indeed, the study of the scientists' observations should help us understand our domestic horse all the more.

Selective breeding does not affect the natural reflex or

instinct, although it may affect intelligence and physique. If the ultimate leaching out of selectively bred thoroughbred stock is on the racecourse, where the proportionate value of stallions and mares may be increased by sterling perform-ance, the same cannot always be said in general breeding of warm-blooded horses.

Although every effort is made at national and private levels to encourage the breeding of high-quality stock by the expert selection and licensing of stallions, and the granting of premiums to mares and foals, actual performance is not the greatest measure of importance in the life of the average riding horse. It is only when one considers activity in relation to actual ability, such as dressage, three-day eventing or show jumping, that performance plays an important role and increases material value as far as the individual is concerned. This is despite the fact that the star performer is often a gelding and therefore incapable of passing on its strengths.

In attempting to breed for superb conformation, intelli-gence, stamina, soundness of bone and wind, utility and beauty, the mating of one horse possessing these qualities to another equally endowed, or the crossing of champion with champion, in no way guarantees offspring with the same high qualities.

Often the combination of an ugly mare and a beautiful stallion, or vice versa, will produce either beauty or success, or both. But one thing is certain: beautiful or ugly, cham-pion or failure, the end product will need to make a living within the protective limits of an equine social system, be it Shetland pony, thoroughbred, Przewalski, or hideous misbreed of unsuitable parents. True natural selection is reserved to the wild, where only the fittest survive.

Captured wild or primitive horses allow themselves to be domesticated fairly easily, which may be explained by the fact that they suddenly become isolated from their herd, without status and therefore without orientation. Curiously enough, it may be concluded that the process of breaking them, unpleasant though it may be in itself, creates both a new social order and security. The breaker becomes the higher rank 'horse' by substituting the missing herd leader. If suitably handled and gentled, the animal will accept its human master as higher in rank than itself, and, if well treated, well fed and watered, will adjust to the new situation.

It is not much different in the case of the domestic horse, except that life is made easier by the presence of traditional or inbred domesticity, which precludes flight orientation, although not flight reflexes, at the outset, together with the advantage of familiarity with human beings. Breaking should be unnecessary because by proper management, as I shall explain, the horse will have been 'broken' at two to three days of age, when it learned to be led from the first moment that it followed its dam out of her box. If possible, this should be the first lesson in domestication. How this is done will be described shortly.

The use of the sense of smell, it would appear, tells the horse whether or not another horse or a human being is acceptable to it. I have repeatedly observed that if a horse does not take up my scent at great length and in detail, that horse will have little, if anything, to do with me. But once the animal is allowed to make its own approach in the way it wishes to do so – without the human interference of rebuffing it and trying to shorten the procedure into what is considered sufficient – it will invariably accept and recognise that person. Some of these inspections are, to say the least, intimate from the human standpoint, but from the horse's point of view, that is no standpoint at all. It is we who must attempt to think like a horse, because a horse cannot think as we do. It is worth remembering that once the horse has made an intimate and detailed study of a person, it is rare that the animal will bother to repeat it.

Such physical scentings are extremely delicate, as well as sensitive, and the horse will not attempt to bowl one over, which is what people seem to be afraid of. The animal has no intention of causing even the slightest injury, so there is simply nothing to fear. I will allow any horse to make such an inspection, be it stallion, gelding or more, and I do so in the certain knowledge that I will be able to approach it any time in the future with complete safety.

The mere fact that I have permitted the animal to inspect me does not mean that I am subsequently going to allow it to take liberties, or get the upper hand. On the contrary, it is I who will get the (quiet) upper hand because the horse now knows me and will do as I ask. For example, an animal which has become accustomed to putting up defences against anyone entering its box, will not do so any more with me and, indeed, its permissiveness through recognition not only by sight, but also by scent, will run through the line of its management.

Deep affection is shown by the horse resting its head on the human shoulder. This is equivalent to its laying the head on the back of another equine friend. It may also press its nose against the hollow of the shoulder, the lips relaxed and the teeth showing, while the expression in the eyes assumes a sleepy or droopy look. Such demonstrations may last for half a minute or even longer and are never discouraged under any circumstances.

Demonstrations of affection are shown by my mare, Tirade, and are usually reserved for the loose-box. She will sidle up, if the mood takes her, and push her head against my chest or shoulder; or she will drop her head to the level of my waist in the hope that I will scratch her poll or just behind her ears and cheeks. Alternatively, she will raise her head high if she wishes to have the hollow under the jawbone stroked, or rest her head on my shoulder if she wants to have her throat rubbed and scratched down to the level of her chest. Firm scratching of the chest muscles, the inner tops of the forelegs, or both, is greatly enjoyed. The eyes will half close, the ears will relax and the lower lip will push forward and droop.

It might be dangerous to attempt these things with entires, and some care should be taken with mares because they, too, can be unpredictable, but the latter are quite safe when they are the initiators of the contact. A person should never

force himself upon a horse; nor should very close relationships with colts be attempted. I once treated a colt for a
rather severe leg injury and it became attached to me and
very familiar. I knew that it would never injure me inten-
tionally but I had to draw the line when it attempted to play
with me as it would with another of its kind. An eight-
month-old colt, advancing on its hind legs and wanting to
put its forelegs on my shoulders to wrestle, is more than a
handful. Neck shaking and butting can also be dangerous
and far too forceful for an ordinary person to cope with. I
firmly discourage such acts.

Shows of affection can be extremely physical indeed,
especially when they involve rubbing with the head which
can easily throw a person off his feet. But care must be
taken here, for a flat rebuttal of such advances is out of the
question if a lasting personal relationship is to be established.
The animal has to be dissuaded gently in order to avoid
causing actual offence. Rebuffed animals do feel slighted,
even hurt, and are quite liable to sulk and refrain from
making further advances. The only people who may find
the foregoing statement funny will be those who have never
really observed their animals closely.

Rubbing the nasal bone and the front of the proffered face
up to the forehead with the flat of the hand, or scratching
in the hollow under the jaw, are accepted as signs of recipro-
cation. Quite hard pinching of the skin from the withers
down along the slope of the shoulder, or exactly along the
line of the deltoid muscle, is usually greatly enjoyed as it
corresponds to the nibbling and combing with the teeth of
another horse. About half a minute of such pinching, or
combing with the fingernails, is enough, the pleasure given
showing in the animal's facial expression and the half closing
of the eyes and relaxation of the ears. The horse may return
the compliment by gently combing the shoulder or arm.

I have already mentioned that the handler becomes the
substitute for the higher-ranking horse in the herd. In a
word, the human, woman or man, becomes the leader of
the limited social group and is capable of keeping the various

group members in their place. The establishment of this
control is relatively easy, in that the human becomes the
superior of the lead horse of the existing social unit, and in
having absolute control of the one, automatically has control
of the others.

In human–horse friendship, or even attempted friendship
on the part of the animal only, acceptance by the human
will encourage the same demonstrations that will be found
amongst horses: mutual greeting by nose to nose touching
and nostril blowing, attempts to groom, shows of affection
by nipping and nibbling, the resting of the head on the body
of the other, and the scenting of the handler's body.

My mare, Tirade, admittedly different from any of the
other horses I know because of her education from an early
age, manifests recognition of the various people in her life,
first vocally and then by degrees of acceptance of the person.
She has different vocalisations for different people, or if you
prefer, different ways of greeting, which would tend to
confirm personal recognition rather than general greeting.

Her order of precedence in shows of affection is as
follows: myself first; her erstwhile rider and friend, Monika,
second; my wife third; and Frau Heller, who feeds her every
morning, fourth.

The vocalisation differs. There is a general crying out as
one of the above leaves the house and makes for the stable
yard, a distance of fifty or sixty yards. This is a loud cry
from the loose-box and is a request for whoever it is to
come along and greet her. She reserves a fairly loud whinny
followed by little whickerings for me, as I approach the
stable, and will stretch her neck in greeting as I come close.
If so inclined, she will bury her face in my hands or under
my jacket when I come into the box. Monika would be
greeted in much the same manner, and the mare, as often
as not, would rest her jaw on her shoulder and snuffle about
under her ear. If I happened to be in the box and Monika
came along, Tirade would rush to the door and wait for the
girl's arrival, but once the two of us were together, she
tended to devote more attention to me. This is probably

because she regarded me as dominant to Monika in the herd order and to everybody else. However, the trust and friendship between Monika and the mare were such that the girl could do pretty much as she liked, and was once disco-vered at eight-thirty in the morning on her return from a holiday, sitting in Tirade's box entertaining her by singing and playing to her on the guitar, while the mare enjoyed her breakfast.

Frau Heller and my wife (I put them in order of who is the more regular visitor to the mare) are greeted in their own individual ways. The former with whickerings, the latter with a soft little voice, or a loud call. My wife, who is a busy person, only looks after Tirade when I am away, taking over the final visit of the day and closing up for the night.

My step-granddaughter is accepted on a par with my Labrador bitch, Tatja. Before she knew any better, the child used to beat the mare on the face with her small open hand, but the mare always came down to her, as indeed she still does. Children seem to occupy a privileged position where domestic animals are concerned, and are allowed to do things that no adult would get away with.

Tatja is accepted in her own right and is welcomed inside the box. I used her in an experiment when she was a pup, and held her up to the mare to be sniffed. Dogs and horses should be able to live together without any problems, but what I wanted to learn concerned the dog more than the horse.

Tirade regarded Tatja as her property and allowed her the run of the box. The mare used to welcome her with lickings and blowings, would comb her with her teeth, or even lift her by the loose skin above the tail or back. The friendship persists today although the bitch will no longer roll on her back to have her belly licked as she used to.

The pony filly, Leila, is also on good terms with Tatja, who is unafraid of her, but Leila will make passes at my son's bitch, Athena, who is a little uncertain but chases her because of this. The pony will lash out with her hind legs, or lower her head and go for the dog, but in each case it is quite obvious that she is either playing or warning off. The pony will allow both dogs into her box at feeding time, although there is no close contact.

Friendships between domestic horses can be very close and sincere. Vavra comments that friendships between mares are the most steadfast amongst the horses he has observed, and states that such friendships are most clearly defined in herds consisting solely of mares. This contrasts with the more casual relationships existing between them where the sovereignty of the herd stallion puts all other relationships in the shade. But, he states, jealousy and possessiveness also play an important role in equine relationships.

I have not personally had the opportunity of observing wild conditions, and my experience of horses is confined to keeping mares, but it seems logical that members of a stallion's harem would not form close bonds of friendship with each other. They would be in season at different times, or coming into season, or in foal; all preoccupations which might well distract from the formation of close friendships and foster rivalries.

Horses not only show jealousy *inter se*, but also where people are concerned. In such cases, outbreaks of jealousy vary in intensity according to the relationship between horse and person. A horse kept alone will rank the humans that play a part in its life, without necessarily displaying jealousy. However, an animal with a jealous disposition will go so far as to engage in threat displays if the 'lower ranking' human appears to be paying too much attention to the 'higher ranking' one.

That horses rank people was made quite clear to me when I took in an old dressage horse named Adonis, for a period of six weeks when Tirade was away on a training course. He accepted me immediately and I had no trouble with him whatsoever. He also accepted the other people around him, showing varying degrees of tolerance. However, when his owner visited him on a couple of occasions, he became immediately jealous and possessive of her and threatened me. But as soon as she had left the yard, he was all over me again. He showed the same behavioural pattern in relation to myself when his owner was not about, and would engage in a series of threat displays directed against anybody who happened to visit his box in my company. But he would accept the same people when I was not present. If a number of people were about, and I was with them, he would come to me and threaten the others. It was clear that he had established a very definite hierarchical system in his own mind and was prepared to put it into effect.

The establishment of a hierarchical system *amongst humans* seems to be natural to a horse that is kept in isolation from its own species. How the animal behaves towards the various people depends upon its personality. Tirade has also ranked her people, but this is shown differently because she tolerates all at the same time. Devoting her attention to the main person in her life she may ignore the others, or will show her favour to one after the other, according to her humour – or whether one of the persons concerned has something to eat in his hand. However, it used to be the case that my presence anywhere within scent or sight range, would upset her concentration while being ridden and she would become difficult.

I sent Tirade away during the summer of 1982, which was the reason, or one of them, why Adonis, universally called Ado, came to me. Tirade went to Herr Trott's small stud farm – from which Leila was to come – in Monika's care. The object was that she should learn something under the tutelage of a good young riding mistress, who had herself learned from Dr Reiner Klimke. I knew how Herr Trott kept and handled his stock and therefore had no hesitation in letting Tirade go there, or Ado come to me. A secondary consideration was that the mare should learn to get along with other horses. Naturally dominant, she showed little inclination to treat other horses with anything but contempt, either ignoring them completely, or threatening or kicking out at them.

She was assigned to an indoor box whose only view was

one of the other horses, thus forcing her to accept communal life. She must have sorely missed her own box with its view of the yard and the constant comings and goings of cars and people, but she had Monika, who both rode and looked after her. As part of the deal, Monika also assisted with other horses in the yard and this incensed Tirade, who regarded Monika as her personal property. As a result she would put on great shows of jealousy and hammer at the sides of her box as soon as her friend went to look after the other inmates of the stable, or ride them out for exercise.

Out in a small paddock in the company of another much larger and dominant mare, Tirade would jostle her and push her out of the way and whenever I came to visit, refused to allow the other mare to come near me, or allow me to give the 'rival' as much as a caress. The other mare never attempted to dominate in my presence, neither threatening nor pushing to try to get at whatever I might have in my hand. I found this particularly interesting because, so I am told, whenever the two were turned out together, the older mare had the edge on Tirade when it came to dominance. This seemed to confirm observations that I had made with other domestic horses in relation to dominance by age in the social order.

Tirade's first displays of jealousy came with the introduction of the pony, Leila, with whom the normal fight for higher rank was inevitable. I kept the two apart, in facing paddocks, for three or four days after I first put the pony out to grass. They looked at each other with some interest, scented, but showed no eagerness to get together as many horses would in a similar situation. When I judged the time to be right, I introduced the pony into Tirade's paddock. Tirade immediately went for her, ears flattened and neck outstretched, her teeth bared. She chased the pony, but the latter would not be subjugated and lashed out, landing a sharp kick on the mare's shoulder, causing an injury. Tirade immediately turned on her forehand, but missed her mark. The two weeks that followed were uneasy. On one occasion when Leila came over to me at a trot, Tirade went for her and met her frontally at such a pace that the two reared up, and the situation might have been serious had I not intervened. Threats and lashings out were frequent. The two would graze far apart. Then, as time passed, they gradually began to get closer in an uneasy peace.

Tirade would not accept the presence of the filly because the mare was jealous of her. There were several reasons for this. The filly would come up at a trot as soon as she saw me appear and would naturally be made much of. I had to bring the pony out every day to put her in the paddock, and Tirade resented this. Tirade would see me grooming the pony in the yard or going into the pony's stable, and she resented that as well. The result was her refusal to have any contact with what she obviously considered a serious rival. The mare's attitudes were so plain to see that I hesitated in beginning the programme of education that I had mapped out for the pony, and at first confined myself to teaching stable manners, hoof-picking and so forth, all done out of sight of the mare.

What became interesting, was the mare's change of attitude towards me. In not accepting the filly, she rejected me and, to a very minor extent, her rider Monika. The main rejection was of myself and she showed this rather as a human might by ignoring me. She sulked, refused to come to hand and if approached, would turn and walk away. Her coolness, if we may describe it in human terms, was extended to her stable behaviour by either ignoring me and standing listlessly when I entered the box, or by showing me her posterior.

Of course it could not last, and, in time, I was able to convince her that there really was no change. What was thought-provoking, though, was the response to the methods that I used to prove to her that Leila was, and is, second-ranking. I decided to show preference on every occasion and to back this up with a great deal of personal contact. She was also taken out for 'social' walks, during which she was allowed to graze. It took about a week to impress upon her that life had not been radically changed because of the pony's arrival. Apparently satisfied, she changed her attitude towards the filly. Even today, there is no close friendship, although they keep together and will not quarrel when hay is put down for them out of doors during hard weather. An undercurrent of mutual mistrust still exists at the time of writing, some eight months after their introduction to one another.

It has to be said that at no time was the filly rebuffed by us, but I made every attempt to bring the two animals close to each other. This was especially so when water was brought to the paddock at midday. Each horse has its own bucket, and interestingly enough, makes for the bucket from which it is accustomed to drink when outdoors. Tirade's bucket is grey and Leila's bucket black, and both horses will unfailingly go to the colour assigned to them. No attempt is made to drink out of the other's bucket; each will wait for her own to be filled. I had not thought that this was possible in the case of horses, although our Labrador dogs certainly recognise their own feeding bowls by colour. Apparently the same rules apply.

All horses are subject to an hierarchical social system in which each member of a herd or group fills a specific place. According to Vavra, even the weakest and most oppressed member of a herd is offered the protection from strangers and animals of prey by the herd stallion and the other strong horses.

The so-called pecking order first observed by Schjelderup-Ebbe amongst fowl and more correctly described as 'ranking order' amongst large animals by Lorenz[3] appears to be common to horse herds. The pecking order is enforced with a greater show among males, whereas mares are more subtle in their display, which may require no more than the rolling of an eye or the twitch of a tail to put the object of displeasure to flight.

One of the tenants on my estate keeps a number of horses and ponies that are in no way associated with our own. They have been extremely useful as study objects and observation of them has clearly shown the establishment and acceptance of rank, as well as their division into groups. I became interested in one group of eight animals living together in an open stable and their behaviour when released into the meadow.

Although relatively sociable when together, they promptly divided into two groups, each with its own leader. One was a Shetland pony that had been gelded late, and the other a mare. Each would get its group together shortly after random release, and move away from the other, keeping a sizeable distance from the rival group during the course of the day. Intrusion into the group by a member of the rival set would immediately cause the lead animal to drive it off with a great show of aggression, although the animals knew each other through living together.

Two geldings who shared a box in the stable, separate from the groups mentioned above, would attempt to join one or other of the groups and consequently create a new situation. One of them belonged to the Shetland-led group and would be instantly recognised and greeted as soon as he was turned out, while the second one would attempt to join the pony mare and her followers. He would be challenged immediately by the mare, who would face him with her ears back and her mouth open. They would stand for a moment, forehead to forehead, until the mare squealed, occasionally struck out, then swung around on her forehand in order to present her quarters and deliver a kick with both hind feet. This rebuff would be accepted and the gelding would trot off.

He would then take up a lone position and nibble at the grass for a while before trying to join the Shetland-led group. The Shetland, who had retained all the instinct of a stallion, would move in fast with great hostility and drive the intruder away. But curiously enough, the gelding would also threaten, swing on his forehand parallel to the Shetland, and attempt to deliver a sideways kick. Both actions between gelding and mare, gelding and Shetland, appeared to me to be ritualistic, for in neither case did any of the participants ever land a serious blow. However, in the case of the mare, the gelding accepted the rebuff and would separate from both groups and graze on the periphery of either of them.

Remarkably enough, the stable companion of the rebuffed animal never came to join him out of doors, although he might occasionally go for a gallop in his company, after which he would rejoin the Shetland and his group.

It was obvious that, although sharing the same quarters, both geldings merely practised toleration indoors, as did the groups that they wished to join, but without any social bond. It was equally reasonable to assume that, without man's intervention, both animals, given free choice, would have had no contact with each other. One is put in mind of two boys having to share the same sleeping quarters at a boarding school, tolerating one another from necessity, but making sure they avoided close contact during the course of the day.

Attempts on the part of the horse to assume a higher rank in relation to the humans around it must be put down gently but firmly. The raised finger on the shaken hand is universally accepted as a threat posture; I know no animal, dog or horse, that does not recognise it as such. A very gentle tap with the index and second finger on the nose is also a deterrent, but rank should not be asserted by either shouting or hitting, and the loudest vocalisation may be a sharply spoken 'No', slightly above a conversational tone. Reproof should be instantaneous, but followed by softly spoken words, because the assertion of self on the part of the horse is for an instant only and not remembered by the animal once the impulse that gave rise to it is over. In showing your own 'threat display' and thus asserting your dominant position in the herd, the animal reassumes its proper rank.

Rank is an essential element within the equine social structure. It enables every member of the society to know where it stands and to get out of the other's way. It prevents the individual members of the society from fighting amongst themselves, yet offers the weakest the protection of the strong. It is, according to Professor Lorenz 'a principle of organisation', without which it is not possible for higher vertebrates to develop a more advanced social life. It is not necessary for us to extend this subject, but to recognise its existence and to act accordingly. Acceptance of the fact will allow us to understand what may appear to be unmotivated, or even seemingly unprovoked, aggressive actions on the part of domestic horses. Our aim should always be to understand motivation and not to misinterpret it. In doing so, we will know what to do and so avoid spoiling or upsetting the animals we are handling.

References

1. VAVRA, R., *Pferdestudien*, Co-Libris Verlagsgesellschaft, Munich, 1979.
2. ZEEB, DR K. *Wildpferde in Dülmen* (4th edition), Hallwag Verlag, Bern and Stuttgart, 1974.
3. LORENZ, PROFESSOR DR K., *On Aggression* (notes 6 and 7, Bantam Matrix Editions, 1969.

CHAPTER 2

Horse Keeping Considered

SUCCESS IN HANDLING depends to no small extent on how the horse is kept. This particular chapter deals with the horse kept alone – its living conditions, the superficial psychology, the keeper's attitudes, as well as western attitudes towards horses, all of which go deeper than the mere keeping and feeding of an animal.

Any domestic animal is wholly at the mercy of the person who keeps it. It is he who determines the course of its destiny during the time he is responsible for it, even to the point of deciding to have it put down. Except for any of the natural defences the animal may have recourse to in order to try and protect itself – and even these may be fully misunderstood – the creature is helpless.

If we wish to face up to the enormity of this statement, then we have to make it clear to ourselves that in owning an animal, we load ourselves with a moral obligation towards it. I never consider that I 'own' an animal – although I may do so legally – but rather that it is 'in my care'. If I am not prepared to assume the inherent responsibility of looking after it properly, then I am morally obliged to see that those who are charged with doing so by me fulfil their obligation. This is especially so in the case of a single horse.

Seeing that your horse is properly looked after if you are paying somebody to do the work for you, is as necessary as doing the job successfully yourself, as shown by the following story which I have been permitted to quote: Diana Tuke relates in her book, *Horse by Horse*[1], how she acquired her thoroughbred mare Galavant. The mare had been out at livery and the owners, from whom Miss Tuke purchased the mare, had not seen her from 'April until August'. This was the result.

> Seldom have we been more shattered on entering a box, for the dark-brown mare of 15 hands 1 inch stood dejected and miserable with her head low on the ground and every bone in her skinny body sticking out through her tight skin – even the heads of the vertebrae were in outline, making her more fit for a veterinary student's model than anything else. Her forelegs were covered in oozing cuts. One horrified look and I turned away in bitter disappointment, but was stopped by a very slight movement of the mare's head. Compelled by an inner force I went back and examined her inch by inch, for as a whole she was too ghastly. As I did so, I realized that here, if I could ever reclaim her, was another top class mare and that she was coming home.

Nobody knows how often this kind of thing happens, or how many horses suffer the misery of lack of love and care. The one is as bad as the other. It is not anthropomorphic to state that animals, especially those belonging to the higher orders, require love in order to flourish. I am sure that Miss Tuke's success in reclaiming her mare – the photographs throughout her book speak for themselves – was as much due to the love she gave to her as to the technical excellence of painstaking and accomplished horsemastership.

Not every story ends so happily for horse and new owner, nor is every unhappy horse so grossly neglected, but there are enough borderline cases. Quite apart from actual physical neglect of the animal itself, many are kept in poor stables that are badly lit, unhygienic, badly drained with filthy bedding and not enough headroom. Or there are those that are left out on deplorable pieces of ground, on waste plots, in every kind of weather, to pick up what they can amongst the refuse.

I am often struck by how little thought is given to the spiritual welfare of horses, both in well-kept stables and poor ones. I intend to re-examine this subject here in order to drive the point fully home.

The problem facing every horse kept in a stable where it can see other horses, is that it is with, but not a part of, a sort of herd with which it has little contact. It neither is, nor has to accept, a dominant horse. It occupies its own stall or loose-box and is alone. The result must be frustration, which may well account for the behaviour of many difficult animals. Horses are contact animals and life within a herd brings out strong mutual likes and dislikes, friendships and loves. That these will be readily established when individuals are put out together, is all too easily seen. Immediate and natural sequences of events will almost instantly take place, and these are the establishment of an order, the making of friends, the biting or threatening of other members of the group if these happen to displease. The dominant horse does not necessarily have to be a stallion; an experienced mare will often take the lead.

Nose touching, mutual scenting, mutual caressing and comforting amongst friends, mutual protection from flies, and closer contact by laying the head on the back of another just behind the withers, are always to be seen in a group or a herd. Society is all, and the establishment of the society and its order is one of the prime concerns of any group of strange horses coming together. But, and this is so often forgotten, skin contact is important and necessary.

Therefore, proximity in a stable, but no direct contact, must be frustrating in the extreme to an animal that will get to know all its fellow stable inmates by the scent they give off.

The lone horse is isolated from this. It can, if it has the temperament, become accustomed to its own company. It overcomes its problem by accepting the human as its herd, or family, and is generally submissive to the human's leading position.

Not too long ago, my wife and I visited a remarkable equine centre which had obviously been built with extensive funds. It has a splendid indoor school, perfectly equipped, a marvellous passage leading from the school to the stables, all paved with non-slip bricks. Tall windows gave light to the passage, near the end of which were two small stabling areas to the left, each with about eight to ten boxes, and two bigger stabling areas to the right, containing considerably more boxes. All the stables had first-class facilities. Two rows of boxes faced each other in each of these rooms. Lighting was from large overhead windows. At the very end of the passage and to the right, a large door gave access to a huge yard, where trailers and horseboxes were parked. This was surrounded by a number of other buildings and paddocks.

Although the whole complex was impressive, I had misgivings about the stables and paddocks. The horses were almost hermetically sealed off from the living world. Their only view was of other inmates in the opposite boxes or by squinting through the windows of the indoor stable doors onto the passage. There were two paddocks behind the great windows that formed one side of the passage to the school. Two sides of each paddock were made up of the blank walls of buildings, the others of stout post and rail fencing. There was one horse in a paddock when we were there and this animal pressed its nose to the glass of the window when I put my hand on it. It could only see me indistinctly.

This whole set-up might be splendid for the human, but, to my mind, not for the horse. I cannot be convinced that a horse feels well in such surroundings. Even one kept under less favourable conditions may be better off than one which is put away and subjected to boring surroundings, however perfect, with hours of standing in its box and only a daily

37

ride or paddock freedom to relieve the day. The higher the intelligence of an animal, the greater the danger of boredom, which leads to vices.

I once made a study of what I described as 'boredom paths' made by isolated animals in paddocks, this also included what I call 'waiting areas'. These boredom paths only exist along the paddock sides nearest to any kind of traffic, almost invariably terminating in waiting areas where the animal stands hopefully until something or somebody comes along. I then made the discovery that the paths and waiting areas virtually vanish as soon as another horse is introduced. Even if the two animals do not get along well together, the grazing pattern changes, the hinterland is fully used and overgrazing near the original path abandoned.

Although we may not like to accept such a point of view, horses are our captives even when they have been born and bred domestically. This does not entitle us to misuse them, to enslave them, or to keep them as prisoners in a cell, no matter how luxuriously it may be appointed. Our job is obviously that of making them what we believe to be happy, which is not, I feel, a concept they would be able to understand in our terms. While we may not be able to do so on *their* terms, we can at least see to it that they lead some sort of individual life which is varied.

I see great danger in any preconceived notions, or in compartmentalising our attitudes towards, or our treatment of, any living creature. Although we may follow the Pavlovian findings and train by conditioning reflexes only, getting good results while doing so, something is missing. In doing so exclusively, we would leave little room to approach the animal and explore either soul or individuality, both of which appear to exist to a very large extent.

I have always been concerned with the mental as well as the physical development of my animals, extending my observations and experiments to those that have come under my care from time to time. I am convinced that, if left all day to itself in a stable, the horse has every reason not to develop its mind and so become dull. A human being locked away in a cell would suffer much the same fate.

Boredom and loneliness present their problems especially where isolated horses are concerned. The appearance of either should be looked for and speedily dealt with. In my experience the more a horse sees and experiences, the more it is handled and the greater variety of action brought into its life, the less the danger of it acquiring vices, which are really deviations from the normal equine behavioural pattern.

The size and quality of living accommodation greatly facilitate the manner of handling and influences the mental health of the animal. A salt block goes a long way towards preventing an inclination to crib or to windsuck, because a horse will bite on it, enjoy it and play with it. The position of the loose-box in relation to the yard is also important. Even if there is no Dutch door, a largish window allowing a view, preferably one of an area where some sort of activity takes place, should exist in any stable. As we know, this is not always the case and frequently cannot be provided. While I do not favour stalls, because the animal is forced to face a blank wall, there is no doubt that a proper stall is preferable to a cramped and low-ceilinged box.

The animal should be able to move freely about in its box without bumping against the walls. A cramped box not only causes the horse discomfort but is more difficult to keep clean, as the horse will be forced to trample its own droppings into the straw bed which it has wetted with its own urine. It will consequently mulch all three and make for less straw economy. A large box will permit the horse to deposit its droppings in an area of its choice, leaving the rest of the straw clean. I usually take the first droppings of a horse new to a box and deposit them in one corner throughout a day and have found that the animal will generally follow up by leaving most of its droppings near enough to this site. If weather conditions demand that I leave a horse in the box all day, all droppings are deposited in one place, since they will be cleared away three or four times each day.

I have my own theories about box construction, as I

have about most things, and put them into practice by constructing my own box to suit what I believe to be a horse's requirements. Tirade's box, which is 14 feet by 13 feet with the ceiling nearly 15 feet from the floor, allows the mare to go for a walk around it when she has to remain indoors. It is equipped with a Dutch door and two windows. The top halves of both windows are open winter and summer. The top half of the door is left open during the summer and early spring and autumn months, but is closed when there is a south or east wind, or when the temperature falls below zero degrees Celsius. The top half of the door and one of the windows overlook a large yard, with other stables to the right, and a house facing. This allows the mare to watch the comings and goings in the yard.

Although my grandparents were considerable horse people, my first contact with the horse took place in my uncle's stables where his carriage horses were kept. I used to be allowed to spend much time there and was greatly encouraged by my aunt who had been an accomplished four-in-hand driver and an excellent horsewoman to boot. I learned much from their coachman, and this included not merely pair driving, but almost everything else to do with 'his' horses. By the time I was old enough to take a real interest, my grandfather was dead, the horses gone, the house sold and my grandmother had moved away.

But unless I am gravely mistaken, my grandparents, as indeed my uncle and aunt, belonged to a generation which regarded their horses as utility creatures, there to be ridden or to draw their carriages. Even my grandmother, friend and pupil of the great James Fillis and erstwhile European dressage champion in the Haute Ecole, probably never did much more than caress her animals or take up the reins in her accomplished little hands. There were Piggot, the coachman, and his grooms to care for, feed and prepare the horses. Nor, as far as I can remember, did my uncle ever visit his mews in my presence.

It is true that western man prizes his dog and is closer to it than he is to his horse. His reason for being so is similar to the reason why the Arab or Turkoman has an equally close relationship with his horse, since the cause is basically the same. The dog shares the white man's life, lives on intimate terms with him in his dwellings, is his companion when he goes out walking or hunting and rides with him in his car. Not so his horse. It lives away from him in its stable to be taken out and used at will. Very often, the stable is far from the owner's home and the animal is looked after by somebody else, the owner only visiting it when he has the time to do so. The master is frequently only interested in keeping a horse for his pleasure, is more concerned with his own art, or lack of it, when riding, than with the personality and needs of the animal itself. Really close contact between horse and owner is rare.

Not so the Arab or the Turkoman. Schiele, in his book *Arabiens Pferde*[2], describing the relationship between Bedouin and horse, tells us that the mare was numbered as a member of the family and allowed to come into the tent with her foal when nights were cold. One spoke to her as one spoke to another human being. Things are different today, but this custom still exists here and there. The Turkoman still takes the foal into his 'jurt', where it grows up with his children and as a consequence of which becomes extremely devoted as a grown-up animal.[3]

It is feared that modern conditions will change the Oriental way of keeping horses and that the intimate relationship may suffer. The stabled horse is put away only to be taken out at will. Urbanisation is responsible for this, just as the acquisition of a mechanically propelled vehicle and wealth contribute their share. As far as our western civilisation is concerned, the structure of our modern society with its manifold pressures and pursuits, plus the fact that an owner's life or safety in no way depends upon the loyalty of his horse, but rather the other way round, makes the horse a luxury and something of a plaything; even worse, what thinking Germans describe as a 'sports instrument'. But this can, and must, be avoided. It can certainly be avoided by country-living people who are able to keep their animals close by. I know from personal experience what fun it is, and how satisfying, to be fully accepted by one's horses.

My own experiments and methods of handling have proved that trusting and mentally well-balanced horses become basically one-person oriented to such an extent that it is possible to enter their box when they are lying down on the straw and feed them tit-bits without them getting up, or to sit quietly in the straw beside them. They may be ranked on a par with dogs in spite of the famous and much-quoted dicta of an Arabian sheikh at a desert oasis in Egypt that: 'You whites treat the dog as your friend and the horse as your slave. It is the other way round with us Arabs . . . and more proper.' Answering the question whether one could keep both horse and dog as friends with a definite 'No,' he went on to say: 'Every man should own a particular horse that he prizes more than anything else on earth. If he befriends a dog, the horse will probably notice it and withdraw his friendship from the man.'[4]

We should take something of this philosophy to our hearts if we wish to succeed with horses, although it is true that we cannot go the whole way. The sheikh's assertion that you cannot keep both dog and horse as friends is not correct. As I have already mentioned, when my Labrador bitch was a whelp, I held her up to my Arabian mare and allowed the latter to inspect her in great detail. The two became firm friends. This is not unusual, as any horse-and-dog-owning family knows.

The sheikh was expressing something that underlined a culture and a whole way of life. It found its well spring in the life of nomadic or semi-nomadic people, who lived very closely with their animals. There was not only the closeness of necessity, but also the religious foundation as well.

Such people tell almost incredible tales about horses, praising the devotion and the courage that they show, and paying them due reverence. No follower of Mohammed would think of mistreating his horse.

References

1. TUKE, DIANA. *Horse by Horse*, J. A. Allen & Co. Ltd., London, 1973.
2. SCHIELE, E. *Arabiens Pferde*, BLV Verlagsgesellschaft mbH, 1973.
3. MÖRMANN, H. and PLÖGER, E. *Buskaschi in Afghanistan*, Verlag C. J. Bucher, Lucerne and Frankfurt, 1978.
4. MOTTISTONE, LORD, *My Horse Warrior*, Hodder & Stoughton, London, 1934. (Published in Germany as *Mein Pferd Warrior* by Deutsche Verlags – Anstalt GmbH, Stuttgart and Berlin.)

CHAPTER 3

Intelligence and Memory

I HAVE OFTEN HEARD people say that horses are stupid. Asked why the person concerned believes this is so, the reason most often given is that if horses were not stupid they would not allow themselves to be dominated by man. When asked to provide a criterion by which the horse's intelligence is measured, the person is frequently at a loss. Asking if the person has made some sort of a special study, one soon learns that he has not. The statement remains unqualified.

It implies, of course, a certain intellectual arrogance on our part to state dogmatically and in general terms that an animal species has, or has not, got intelligence. If we do so, we are measuring its intelligence, or our concept of the qualities that would give it such, by human standards. Thus, if its behaviour does not fit into our mental picture of what we deem to be intelligent, we pronounce it to be stupid. This is manifestly wrong since we are incapable of entering an animal's mind. We are only able to observe mental reactions and draw from our experience and observation.

It might be reasonably safe to assert that a specific animal is stupid, or reasonably intelligent, or even very much so, because there are great differences in equine individuals. Therefore, the statement that A is cleverer than X is legitimate. But to state that horses as a species are stupid, is not. We may only make a general statement, with reservations, when we have studied one's notes on a cross-section of study objects, examined the work of others and statements concerning their findings, re-examined our own conclusions in the light of them and arrived at what we *may* consider to be a reasonable conclusion. It is therefore only possible to measure the intelligence of a particular animal against the intelligence of other members of its species; for to measure equine intelligence against that of the human is palpable nonsense. It is close to admitting an inability to recognise the difference between chalk and cheese. If we take the mental ability of an extremely intelligent horse and measure it against that of a ten-year-old child, we will find that the horse is a comparatively *backward human being*. But were we to compare human intelligence with some of the more inexplicable equine superiorities and reflexes, we should find the human to be a very *inadequate horse*. Interspecific comparisons leading to generalities have no value. Water and spirit may be bottled and poured, because both are liquid, but the similarity ends there.

Intelligence is intellectual skill, or knowledge and mental brightness. It should not be confused with conceptual thinking which, in the case of horses, is admittedly limited. Wynmalen, author of *Equitation*,[1] discussing the same subject, defines it as 'the capacity of the mind for knowing and understanding', and remarks that it implies 'the faculty of making a reasoned use of physical and mental attributes, and employing means to ends'.

If we accept these definitions, we are able to establish a criterion against which we may come to useful conclusions by study and experiment. Why we should want to do this is self-evident. In educating, handling and training, the intellectual capacity of the individual may not only be used to help us achieve our aims, but, by careful cultivation, be expanded as well as developed. A horse whose intelligence has been furthered and conditioned is easier to teach than one denied that kind of experience. But with or without any form of tampering, equine intelligence, like that of the human, varies between individuals and no amount of conditioning will make a stupid horse any the brighter for it.

My own studies and experiments have led me to the opinion that the average horse is about as intelligent as the average dog, an animal with which it shares the characteristics of excellent memory, some conceptual thinking ability and a willingness to please and learn. In common with dogs, domestic and domesticated horses are primarily one-man, or one-woman, animals. This, together with the circle of their accepted human friends, gives them the basic security they require in order to be spiritually stable and uncomplicated members of society. It is this quality that we may build upon when handling and educating them.

If we are intent on furthering mental capacity and developing it, in order to make use of it, the methods of human approach and handling become of prime importance and even supersede the manner of keeping. Although I have dealt with this under a separate chapter heading, it will suffice to say here that horses enjoying little, if any, warm communication with their owners or keepers, and not much more than visual contact with their equine neighbours, are liable to stultify. It cannot be otherwise with an animal of a highly social nature. Skin contact is necessary.

Horses are possessed of what some people call curiosity; what others, like myself, would term a lively interest and a constant need of information. They want to know what is going on, what things are, how they smell, what will happen if they go near them. They look, they memorize, and will do so repeatedly if in doubt about something. They combine very clearly what is being demanded of them with the situation in which it is being demanded. If their grasp is good and their tutor is explicit, they will learn the fundamentals of anything we try to teach them, with often remarkable willingness, even eagerness, providing we do not make it a bore by senseless repetition.

It is impossible for us to enter into the horse's mind. It is convenient to believe that the animals do not think at all, because a non-thinking entity makes no demands upon our conscience. It is too easy a way out. What is more, such a belief allows us to abandon the animal until we see fit to use it, and to forget it for the rest of the time.

We must always bear in mind that any animal which is living in a state of domestication, even though it has been born to such a state, is living an unnatural life and has to subjugate itself to a human social order. This means that in many respects it has to subdue its natural instincts, to learn new ways of living, and adapt itself to 'new' living conditions upon which its survival depends. It does not apply reason to this process of adaptation, but does so by its self-preservation instinct, like foxes, owls and other small wildlife which live within certain London squares. It does, however, use intelligence to meet most situations. The society into which it has been forced by domestication, being contrary to the animal's natural society, creates problems with which it can only come to terms by its powers of observation, memory, ability to understand and assimilate, and its general intelligence.

Despite all these qualities, it has difficulties in overcoming boredom. Penned or captive animals bore easily, and the horse is no exception. This is something that we should understand and with which we should sympathise. Signs of boredom have to be watched for in the stable *and* in the meadow, especially if a horse is kept on its own. Boredom leads to abnormalities, bored animals will do things they would never do under natural conditions. Examples are feather-pecking amongst pheasants and chickens, which may lead to cannibalism; excessive scratching and excreting by dogs; wind-sucking, weaving, crib-biting or bed– and droppings-eating amongst horses. It is a mistake to believe that a horse, snug and 'happy' in its box, is safe and out of danger. Boredom can best be prevented by variety; the more intelligent the animal, the more susceptible it may be to boredom.

Boredom suggests a mental activity of some kind, because the passage of time, or inactivity, would not become wearisome if there were no mental process. Horses will engage in some form of activity if left on their own and will devise a manner of keeping themselves occupied. I am reasonably sure that cribbing, weaving and other stable vices are due to intelligent horses being confined and not knowing what to do with their time.

I know from experience what a bright horse can get up to when left on its own. My own Arab mare, Tirade, is not only brighter than most horses to start with, but she has become even more intelligent because of her constant handling and contact. If confined to her box for any length of time, she will either become sour and off humour, or she will show her abilities as an escapologist. I cannot remember how many different gadgets I have devised as additional security measures on the lower half-door of her box. She has managed to overcome all of them, except the last. The consistency with which she mastered the problems convinced me that she applied her mind to the task on hand and that none of her escapes were accidental.

A predecessor of hers, Farina, learned how to open the sliding door of her box if the pin was not put securely into the hasp. She would shove against the door, loosen the hasp, open the door with her upper lip – her hand, as I call it – and walk out of the box. I settled down to watch how she did it and discovered that she had observed, and obviously memorised, the movement of my hand – where I placed it when opening the door – because she did exactly the same.

I rate learning by observation as the highest form of mental awareness, because it presupposes direct application of whatever mental prowess there is. Further examples of mental applications were evidenced by the same mare, Farina, and her stable companion, Fricka, who both could untie simple knots while standing at the hitching rail. Again this had not been taught – it is the last thing one would wish to teach a horse – but they had observed the tying, day by day, and could perform the first step of untying, although physically unable to master the second.

Once we have established the existence of intelligence, we can turn our attention to the teaching of language, even in a limited form. Contact with human beings demands communication on both sides. The horse is expected, as a matter of course, to respond to human language, and I have found it interesting to watch the reactions of horsemen when I point out that the learning of language by the animal is an even more remarkable feat than the learning of Chinese, Hungarian or Finnish, all three recognised as amongst the most difficult languages to master, by a human being.

Words and their meanings become clear to animals, provided they are taught properly. Limited vocabularies are assimilated, memorised and subsequently acted upon. This applies to horses, dogs and human infants alike. Although people may throw up their hands in horror at the statement, human infants will react in the same manner as horses and dogs if they are taught much the same basic vocabulary. Were we now to teach a horse, dog or infant to respond in a specific manner to a planned series of grunts and gutturals, then the language learned would be one of grunts and gutturals, with each grunt or guttural representing a 'word'.

There are many people who subscribe to the belief that animals react only to the *tone* of a word and not to its meaning. This is partly true, because words are little more than a formal assembly of tones, arranged to produce a meaning which is generally accepted. Thus, if we attempt to introduce somebody to a new language, we will try to do so with aids, like holding up a spoon and repeating the word 'spoon' until the meaning becomes clear. The same principle applies, only more so, when we teach a very small child.

We use the same technique when trying to teach language to a horse or dog; we employ this demonstrative method, coupled with a word or tone, and hope, by repetition of the act and the word itself, to make the meaning clear to the pupil. Although, strictly speaking, we are conditioning a reflex, I prefer to describe this process as 'action-linking'. It is a handier term, as well as specifying exactly what one does when working with the horse.

If we do not action-link a word, it becomes abstract, like a sound coming from an unidentified source. The word does in fact become a meaningless sound, because, as far as I have been able to ascertain, animals are incapable of understanding abstracts. There is, however, one exception within my experience, and that is the use of the word 'quiet'.

'Quiet' becomes one of the most important and useful words in the equine vocabulary. But communicating the true meaning of this word is more complex, because it is best conveyed by the calm and sureness of the handler in given situations. It is therefore largely tonal and takes on no meaning until the horse learns that it is only used when it is excited or afraid. It is about the only abstract that can be easily taught, because in teaching, I use my own vibrations, or calm, physically, either through the leading rein or by touching the animal with my fingertips.

I obviously teach useful words first. I think that 'come', 'stand', 'forward', 'no', and short sentences, like 'move over' and 'give the head', cover most needs when trying to introduce a foal to human language. I teach 'come' by enticing the animal to come to me for a carrot in the box. Later, when it has learned about the headcollar, I may also pull it gently towards me on a leading rein and give it a reward. The word is important, because the horse should always come when called. I teach 'stand' by denying the pupil forward movement. 'Forward' is taught when leading, and 'give the head' by first putting on the headcollar as gently as I can and by the method suggested elsewhere. Upon this basic vocabulary, all subsequent teaching of words may be made to hinge. The word always precedes the action and is invariably spoken. 'Go back', 'turn around', 'take the bit', 'go to the manger', are examples of short sentences that can be understood and acted upon.

'Make room' or 'move over' are the first basic sentences, taught by gently pressing against the pupil's flank with the fingertips. They are made comprehensible by linking them to an action.

Then, curiously, a non–word, 'B-r-r-r-r', can be taught when lungeing or loose schooling and when the horse is going too fast. All horses appear to react to this one, which I learned when being taught to drive a pair.

However, if a word is used outside the context of a familiar sentence, it ceases to have any meaning, even if spoken in the same tone. If I were to walk into a box and ask the occupant, 'How is your *head* this morning,' I should expect and get no reaction at all. But if I went into the box and said, 'Give your head,' and I had a brush or a headcollar in my hand, the animal, knowing the words, would give its head either to accept the headcollar or to have its face brushed. Head, brush, bridle, headcollar and leading rein are all associated through vision, word and action.

In my yard all objects are named, first shown to the horse, then given it to smell and are only then used. It is doubtful that the animal understands the meaning of the word 'dandy brush', but it will lift each foot readily after one has given it the hoof pick to smell and see. The practice is followed on every occasion.

Certain phrases stick and are acted upon. For example, the old mare Fricka learned to take up her position in front of the manger when told to do so. The box that she occupied, and which is now the home of the pony filly Leila, has a big stone manger at the furthest end, so that one has to pass through the length of the box to get to it. This means that if the horse is very hungry, or greedy, it is liable to bully the feeder in its efforts to get at the food being brought in. The horse must be taught not to push and trample in its eagerness at meal times. The words, 'Go to the manger', would be used and the animal would take up the correct position and wait until the oats were poured into the trough from the measure.

I changed the feeding routine, but about six months after I had done so, I asked Fricka to go to the manger and she went at once. She had neither forgotten the sentence nor the meaning of it. I had no food in my hand at the time, it was merely a test, but the response was immediate. She had acted on the words, not on the sight of food. Obviously, she understood what the manger was.

Tirade responds to the word 'home'. We take off both saddle and bridle at the hitching rail after riding and do not bother to put on the headcollar or use the rein to lead the horse across the yard. She is simply asked to go 'home'. There are times when she decides that this is a bore and wanders off, but normally she will make straight for her box.

'Walk', 'trot', 'canter' are about the last words to be taught, since they represent an activity that will not be asked for from a very young horse until it comes on the lunge. They will be taught at about the same time as 'watch your head', and 'attention', which is a useful word when riding or when doing something in the box that might spook the animal. I usually fluff up and damp the hay in the presence of the horse, who will begin to nibble at it as soon as it is put down. Sprinkling the hay with water is done after it is put down. I call 'attention', and the horse will turn aside until I have finished, returning to the hay when I call out 'O.K.'

Of course the understanding of language, in specific terms, is limited to words that have been taught. Beyond that, the animal reacts to the tone of the spoken sentence. Extraordinary sensitivity to atmosphere and its ability to pick up the vibrations of mood, make it react accordingly. The animals become nervous and excitable if their handler is upset and I only touch upon the subject here, insofar as mood may be communicated by speech. I will discuss it in greater detail, when I come to other forms of communication.

Neither animals, nor very young human beings, think of themselves in the first person singular. Careful observation of my step-granddaughter, Philippa, showed that she did not think of herself in that way until she had passed the age of two and a half years and was able to grasp the fact that adults, in referring to themselves, called themselves 'I'. Inability to communicate the concept would preclude teaching its meaning to an animal. Philippa, who always was quick-minded and reasonably advanced for her age, referred to herself by her given name: 'Lippa wants teddy,' or 'Lippa doesn't want . . .', or whatever the message happened to be. She associated her name with personal identification. It is the same in the case of an animal, which identifies itself with its given name or the name used in relation to it. The name becomes the first person to the animal. Tirade, always called Tina, will come to that name, not her pedigree name, although phonetically the two are not far different.

It is evident that every horse identifies itself with its name which it regards as peculiar to itself. Responses to the name may be vocal even when the familiar voice calling it is out of sight.

Neither of our horses 'speak' English. They have been educated in German and will only respond to known words in that language. Experiments with our Labrador retrievers show that a dog may be bilingual. All our retrievers will answer correctly to English or German. Their brothers and sisters will not and one might as well be crying to the moon to attempt to get one of them to react to an English word, unless it is similar to the same word in German. Consequently 'come' (*komm*) is understood. The horses react to words that are phonetically not too dissimilar, like the example already given, or 'hoof' (German *Huf*). But 'high' (*hoch*) means nothing at all, and the same applies to 'head' (*Kopf*), or 'tail' (*Schweif*, in equine terminology). Attempts made to find responses to 'foreign' words have shown me that even when these are spoken in monotones, nothing but negative responses may be expected. The horse fails completely to understand what is wanted of it.

I have been at pains to teach young people, who are associated with my animals, to talk to them when either handling or riding them. They are always being urged to talk to their mount from the saddle and it is curious how difficult it is to get them to do so. It makes them feel foolish for some reason or other. In this respect, young Jenny is the best of my pupils and, although her horsemanship leaves much to be desired at the present time, Tirade will put herself more readily on the bit when Jenny is in the saddle. I quickly found out that the girl talks to the mare all the time, with the result that the animal relaxes completely. However, this is the use of the human voice as a measure of reassurance and has little or nothing to do with language, or the understanding of it by the animal. It is here that the use of the voice is tonal and equivalent to my talking to an equine pupil that is being lead, lunged or on long reins.

While both horses and dogs may be taught words and made to understand their meanings, the tonal use of the voice cannot be denied or ignored. It plays a major role in daily contact with horses, and it is the TONE of the voice, in conjunction with the words used, which will either pacify or excite the animal, or in certain situations, act as the ultimate form of control. It is the easy and soothing voice level that conveys confidence, or a sense of normality. Excited horses may be 'talked down', even if the talk is gibberish and phrases like 'quite quiet', long programmed into the horse's vocabulary, are used to create the atmosphere.

The almost legendary equine memory can, and should be, used in educating and training horses. But, equally, great care should be taken in doing so. We should make use of the memory in the proper sense and not abuse it in order to form habits that become mechanical. I will only follow the latter course if, for example, I want the horse to stand in the open door of its box until I am ready for it, or if possible, to learn to stand stock still the moment that the rider dismounts or is about to mount; the latter is more difficult than the former, because every horse that is being mounted knows the fun is about to begin and is inclined to move off when the foot of the rider puts weight on the stirrup.

While the memory has its great advantages in teaching

and handling, it can be a terrible boomerang. Mishandling, incidents of deliberate cruelty, or negative experiences of people or places will remain. It should be said that mishandling, within this context, means handling in the wrong way, either by schooling wrongly or even by treating the animal wrongly, although there is no intention of doing it any harm. If we take a simple example, such as putting on the headcollar roughly or thumping the saddle thoughtlessly down on the back, or shouting at the horse if it will not give its feet readily to be picked out, we will have an idea of unintentional mishandling.

Such thoughtlessness, should it occur repeatedly, may well lead to permanent headshyness, or fear of the saddle, or of having the hooves picked up. But teaching the horse something at the same time and always in the same place, may equally be considered mishandling, because the event will be stored in the memory and associated with the time and place, so that the horse refuses to perform what it has been taught anywhere else.

Memory does go beyond such things. Something that the horse found to be pleasant will also be remembered. It will remember places and people, and its way home, should its rider give it liberty to do so. An old servant on this estate, now as dead as the pony that used to be such a friend of his, used to go out on a spree now and then and, quite incapable of driving the animal, allowed it to find the way home. This was much the same with a Dublin milk-delivery horse from whose driver I cadged a lift in my student days. I had brought a girl home in a taxi and could not afford the return fare. With the milk-float driver fast asleep beside me – it was six in the morning, and I was wearing white tie and tails – we moved at a reasonable clip into the city from its outskirts. It happened that there were one or two stopping places on the way. The horse, knowing these, stopped at them, in one case entering a yard. 'The auld horse never forgets,' his driver assured me with pride, before settling back to snooze until the next call. Nor, it must be said, did anybody forget the horse who, on each occasion, was given something good for his trouble.

The great advantages of the memory are displayed when one teaches and then praises when the lesson has been even half learned. Pupils are susceptible to praise and react positively to it. They recognise and remember it, and try to do well the next time the lesson is repeated. The tip of the touching cane (more about which later) reminds and demands without the need to touch after a couple of lessons. The sight of the cavesson and lunge reminds it and because it remembers, the horse will come readily to hand for the work that is going to follow. The fact that we may use words is entirely due to the horse's memory. Indeed, that memory is what makes handling a proposition from the very start.

References

1. WYNMALEN, HENRY, *Equitation*, J.A. Allen & Co. Ltd, London, 1971.

CHAPTER 4

Time, Teaching, Training

TIME plays an almost overwhelming role in anything to do with horses. People who buy a riding horse wish to own a finished product. They want to ride it. Why, otherwise, do they want to own it? The breeder is concerned with selling them the finished product. That is his business. He will either break the animal himself or send it out to be schooled by a professional. A schooled horse commands a better price.

Horses cost money to stable, feed, groom and work with. Few breeders and trainers have the time to take the youngster really in hand between weaning and the time it is broken and backed, but this, of course, is the moment to make the horse. It is doubtful if anyone has time to concern himself with individual psychology. *If* they had the time, *if* they could assess the very individual needs of every horse, then the end product would have to fetch a high price in order to compensate them.

Likely as not, the young animal is allowed to run with its kind until it is ready to be broken and backed, which means that it is more species- than human-oriented. Such a horse, taken away from the group, has to be broken, whereas a youngster who has been the subject of highly individual treatment and attention from, say, the first year and a half of its life, need never be broken, but only backed. It has already been physically, and, above all, mentally prepared for its life's work, and is willing to go along with its trainer.

I own a book – which will not be mentioned in the bibliography – in which there are six photographs, obviously taken on two separate occasions, showing a horse being schooled by a professional. These pictures not only tell a tale, but at the same time explain why many horses are as they are; and that in a negative sense.

Quite clearly, the ideal is to obtain a horse that does not have to be broken and to back it yourself, or to have it backed under your supervision. But it is equally clear that this is not always possible. Many would-be owners haven't got the time, the inclination, the knowledge or the interest to buy a yearling and wait for three years, which time will be devoted to educating the youngster, before they can sit on its back.

To a person like myself who is interested in the horse primarily for its own sake and who is not interested in riding it, the evolution of the young animal into the ultimate horse is by no means restricted by time.

With such fortunate conditions prevailing, it is possible to teach carefully, not to rush the pupil and therefore not upset its nervous system.

No young horse should be asked to carry a rider until it is rising four years of age, and it is even better if it has passed its fourth birthday. There are those who argue that a three-year-old is well up to their weight, and indeed it may appear to be so, but it has to be remembered that the articular portions at the extremities of most long bones are united to the main bone shaft only by cartilage and that solidification does not take place until the young animal is two or even more years of age. As long as this condition exists there is a danger of permanent injury if the animal is overtaxed or overloaded. This may lead to hidden damage that may be the source of trouble later on during the life of the horse. Many animals show defects which are not endemic but which may be traced back to thoughtless or even selfish handling at too early an age.

This must be taken into consideration and, quite obviously, the longer the animal is allowed to develop without any but natural stress, the better it must be. Although it is true to say that a two-year-old is quite capable of carrying some weight – and it may be argued that racehorses do so at this age without apparent ill effect – it is better to start a little late with the rider, than a little too early.

But we are not discussing thoroughbred racehorses here because they are an exception. We are talking about riding horses, average horses that are to become good all-rounders to be hacked, or ridden over country to hounds, or those who may become what I call specialists: show-jumpers, eventers or dressage horses. These are animals which show talent in a particular direction and are subsequently trained to fulfil a function. One has to remember that there is no such breed as a hunter, a show-jumper or a dressage horse or hack, any more than there are breeds of men called lawyer, doctor or coal miner.

Although the knowledgeable may well see the potential in a young animal, the fact of the matter is that the discovery of its particular talent does not really show up until it comes under the rider when, the more talented the rider, the more the horse's own talent will be developed, by which time about nine years have passed since the animal's conception. This is the crux of the matter.

It is quite obvious, even without recourse to the expert literature on the subject, that a horse is as good as its feet and legs. They will bear enough stress throughout the animal's active life as a jumper, eventer, chaser, or even during pleasure riding, without taking on too much too soon. Most horses, when jumping, land with all their weight on one forefoot, usually the right one, which has to take the weight of the animal itself plus the weight of the rider.

59

The old dressage horse, Ado, who was with me for a time and who had been used as a school horse in Dr Reiner Klimke's stable, was the perfect illustration of a horse correct in its legs. He looked like a six-year-old when seen at a distance because of his dry, impeccable legs and was a joy to watch when walking.

The more time allowed in the early natural physical development of a horse's bone and musculature, the longer it will be able to serve its owner. Moreover, physical stress will bring about mental stress, just as easily as cruelty or spiritual rebuffal. One may force the pace in advancing the horse rapidly, but there may be a price to pay, either by building-in hidden physical damages, or instability of character, or by not allowing time to ensure that the lessons are permanently understood.

Human children who are big for their age are often at a considerable disadvantage. They may suffer a good deal from those around them when their real age and the mentality that goes with it is forgotten because of their physical size. They may even be unjustly scolded for defending themselves against the aggressions of smaller companions and be accused of bullying because of it. Adults, teachers and parents expect more than these children can give: 'A big boy like you ought to know better!' Being overtaxed, by reason of their size, may influence every aspect of their lives from table manners to performance in school, or general behaviour patterns.

Young horses suffer from somewhat similar disadvantages. A young horse is a big animal, strong and capable of giving its handler trouble. There is always the danger that its capacity is overrated because of these factors, not by its actual mental and physical age. Thus, adult work may be demanded of a 'child'.

Although it may not achieve it for various reasons, a horse's life *expectancy* is forty years; most horses die between the ages of twenty-one and twenty-seven. By the time the animal is ten years old it has lived a quarter of its life. If we take the life expectancy of a human being on the biblical basis of three score years and ten, the first ten years in the life of a horse may be equated to seventeen and a half years of human life. A two-year-old horse, if we wish to preserve the same age relationship, is therefore equivalent to a 4.63-year-old human child. So, for all its apparent strength, a two-year-old is still a child. And it will behave like one. Young horses are playful, often lacking concentration, imaginative and skittish. They like to fool about. If you take the time to observe them in the paddock, they can be seen enjoying sudden flurries of activity: shying, kicking up their heels and taking fright for no apparent reason. They will react to all kinds of non-existent threats and dangers. Even a seven-year-old will play up from time to time if the mood seizes it.

For those who may have recently come into contact with the horse for the first time and who might be expecting great things of it, I have chosen two development time tracks in order to illustrate how much time is required to develop a horse. The one is an Occidental time track, the other an Oriental one.

Assuming that our young Occidental horse has been well treated and handled during its early days, but that it is started, as so many are, at the age of three years, its life should be somewhat as follows. It will be broken to the bit after it has cut its second teeth and backed after that event. It will be regularly lunged, taught to accept the mounting and dismounting of the rider, and then, after a period on the lunge, will carry a rider for ten to twenty minutes a day, not more, in order not to strain its back. As soon as the horse is capable and willing to carry the rider, its normal development and training as a riding horse begins. There is no need to go into that here as it has nothing to do with the footwork we have been talking about. Suffice it to say that the animal will not be asked to do any hard work until it is five years of age, although the workload will be gradually increased. Now I know of horses that are being asked to do a show season, albeit only at small shows, after their fourth year. That is much too early, especially if they are being asked to jump.

The Oriental horse, and I have chosen the Afghan, which is to be used in a specialised field, starts its career as a three-year-old just as the Occidental one does. It is introduced to the saddle for the first time to begin its training for the game of *Buskaschi*, to which end it must learn the rein aids, speed and manoeuvrability. It will gather its first experience of the incredibly hard game as a four-year-old, when it will be carefully ridden on the periphery in order to train it not to shy away from the general noise and tumult. Should it prove itself, then the trainer will ride it closer to the action, but not into it. At this stage, the pupil is five years old. Thereafter, the training will continue under a more experienced rider. Two years of hard work will follow until the animal, now seven years old, may participate in the game for which it was born and bred.[1]

If we go by the above, we will note how, in both Occident and Orient, a horse is not asked to perform hard work until it is about six or seven years of age. If we allow seven years for the animal to go through childhood and adolescence, we may reckon a further fourteen to seventeen years of work before retiring it at or between the ages of twenty-one and twenty-seven, which seems to be reasonable enough. Although if a horse has not been overstressed, it may be gently ridden for a long time after its twenty-seventh birthday.

The *leitmotif* of this book is to advocate the education and elementary teaching of young horses from a very early age in order to gain time and avoid stress. Quite obviously, the few minutes spent per day with the horse amounts to a good deal of time when spread over years, with the advantage that the animal is fresh when it comes to teaching its work under saddle.

Teaching times should be short. Just how short surprises many, even when re-schooling, in-hand, horses that have been spoiled. Some friends and I had a discussion some time ago on the amount of time that should be devoted to daily lessons when training dogs and horses to be handy. I told them that I seldom went beyond a minute when starting something new. That, I said, was quite enough, although the time may be increased to ten or fifteen minutes later on, when the horse or dog understands. I am, of course, referring to one specific discipline, say, for example, teaching the horse to be whip-wise or to stand. Even then, the allowed minute should be divided into two sessions, in other words, half a minute per session.

One of the arguments offered against my thesis was that, surely, nobody could teach anything in so short a time, and certainly, to prepare a horse for lungeing in order to make it work for five or six minutes during the introductory sessions must be nonsense and a waste of time and effort.

It has to be remembered that a horse is not specifically time oriented, although every animal has a built-in clock governing its general behaviour and movement in a wild or feral state when, through observation over a period, it may be found with reasonable certainty in certain places at certain times. It is especially so with feral swans.[2] The built-in clock may be trained – conditioned – to cover feed times, and this is what is normally done either consciously or unconsciously, thus allowing routines to be changed or established by a horse's keeper.

Notwithstanding this, no animal understands, or can be made to understand, small divisions of time. A minute is therefore a long period. Quite obviously, teaching times, in minutes, are increased as the pupil learns progressively. To increase a teaching time from one to five minutes at a jump by assuming that because your horse now stands for a minute, it can stand for five, would be nonsensical, just as it would be to expect that the lesson involved may be learned within a given space of time related to days.

The human attitude must be adjusted to accept that a lesson is learned *when* it is learned, no sooner and no later and regardless of human time concepts. Although the unit of one minute may pass very quickly and seems to be a short time measure, it can be quite long a period to an animal. To those who argue the period is too short to teach anything – there will probably be many who will do so – I suggest the following experiment. Find a nice level floor, take your watch in hand, wait until the second hand shows the beginning of a minute and stand on one foot for exactly sixty seconds without once attempting to support yourself by any other means. You will most probably find this a strain and difficult. But successful or not, you will come away with an understanding of just how long one minute can be.

Now think of how long the same period is to a dog or a horse when asked to sit or stand still. I am usually very pleased if I can get any untutored horse to stand still for as much as fifteen seconds the first time that I ask it to do so.

It is useless to discuss education and early training without thinking about time. To begin with, it is a mistake to try to fit a horse to man's ambitions by demanding too much too soon. As I have said, we do not, and should not, demand too much of our children and the same rule applies to the horse. But we can, and do, advance our children from infancy by teaching them elementary disciplines and the elementary necessities that allow further development and integration with the human system we like to call society.

I have suggested no times in relation to the learning of disciplines and lessons, and have been most careful to avoid saying that the horse should learn something taught to it within the framework of a specific time space. It would be foolish to do so. I have stressed elsewhere that each animal is highly individual and that this individuality must be carefully studied. There is not only the question of individuality to be thought about, but also the matter of personal talent, aptitude and intelligence, for, as I have pointed out, there are stupid, clever and very clever individuals. In this respect, there is no such animal unit as a standard horse.

Fortunately, there are many excellent professionals who think as I do. A friend of mine who is deeply involved in the horse-racing world, took me along to visit the half-sister of his filly, then in training in Newmarket. The filly in question was in training in Hanover and her trainer, Herr

Kurt Lepa, introduced her to us with justifiable pride. As we went into her large box, she came up to greet him first and then did the rounds of the three of us. She was a very elegant animal, not in the least bit nervy, very gentle and obviously well handled.

'This,' said the trainer, 'is a filly that ought to do extremely well, providing nobody is allowed to pull her to pieces.'

I immediately wanted to know what he meant by 'pulling her to pieces'. Did he mean riding her too hard, or what? He quickly made it clear that he was talking about the animal's character, her evident sweetness, her trust and her calm. She must be properly handled and ridden. He told us that he would not allow anybody to turn her into 'an unmanageable bundle of nerves'. I felt excused for remembering what I had seen about half an hour earlier in the ring at the race meeting which was the reason for our being in Hanover that day. A fighting, rearing, nervous animal that forced its jockey to slip off the moment after he had been put up, so unmanageable was it. Or was it simply that its girth was too tight, or was something under its saddle cloth to upset it? I hoped it was not the nature of the horse itself.

The racehorse Golden Cygnet was another example of good and understanding handling and management. He began his distinguished career by being difficult and almost impossible to ride. To quote his trainer, Mr O'Grady, 'So difficult was he that in some stables he might never have been ridden at all and we only succeeded with him because of the ability of some of my very good lads.'[3]

Both the trainers mentioned are first class in their approach, as well as capable of understanding the spiritual side of the animals in their charge. This is possibly the attitude of the majority of good trainers. If their horses do not come up to expectations on the racecourse, they will probably be usable and re-trainable as riding horses when sold as such after a period of rest.

Where, then, do horses go wrong? I believe that in saying how one should handle one's personal horse, I have also given the reasons why an individual may be spoiled through being forced or brought on too quickly or improperly handled. I have the feeling that most of the spoiled horses I have come up against are more the products of non-professionals who, having bought a horse, did not have the knowledge or the interest to bring it on from the moment that they bought it, simply because they regarded it as a finished product. This is very often the case. Even a relatively accomplished animal must be worked with, and on, if it is going to give of its best, and its best is relative.

My personal experience has taught me that even my carefully handled and schooled horses require constant education and development once they come under the rider. The preliminary schooling in-hand and subsequent schooling under the rider are a continuous process and interlock. Both are closely bound to, and conditioned by, the temperament of the horse and the understanding of that temperament by the individual who wishes to educate or re-educate it. Temperamental differences amongst horses are so wide as to demand much study. There are horses who take their lessons so much to heart that they worry about them, just as there are those who are difficult to teach. There are others who merely play about and try to get their own way, while there are some that have to be taught how to concentrate.

An individual with concentration problems requires time in the teaching, as well as the need to make the whole of its working life interesting and varied. Sometimes, painful human parallels are encountered.

Training, which always sounds important because there is a tendency to associate it with the racecourse and early mornings on the gallops, is no more than getting the horse fit to do its job. Every horse that has a job to do should be in some sort of training, which is another way of saying that it should be physically fit. Thus, the degree of fitness varies. The pleasant hack, the dressage horse or the horse used for hunting, will not need the same pitch that a polo pony, a racehorse or a three-day-eventer must have. Nor will the feeding be the same.

Horses, in common with humans, become soft, and an animal that is constantly grass kept, or kept in the box and exercised for an hour a day, is a bit like a human who goes for a walk having spent most of his day in the office, or plays a game of mild tennis in order to keep fit. Nobody would expect such a human to be capable of competing in high-class athletics. The horse has to be made tough and its stamina built up before anything may be demanded of it. This is so obvious that I am almost ashamed to mention it – but it is a fact that horses are damaged every year by having demands made of them which they are in no condition to meet.

We must always remember that a horse will go as long as we ask it to do so. It will literally go until it drops dead in its tracks. I know of three horses that collapsed and died during two drag hunts one year because their owners, through innocence or ignorance, took them out, unfit, for a day's hard work at the beginning of the season.

Unless I am advancing work on long reins or repeating lessons, my work stops when the four-year-old comes under the rider. The young horse is usually in pretty good condition by the time I have finished with it and it is ready to be built up thereafter under the saddle. I am then only concerned with working with horse and rider, the first year of work being carefully planned and supervised.

What the pupil has learned in-hand is then furthered by the rider, the preliminary work being concentrated on the response to the aids in order to ensure immediate reaction to the leg aids and to the preservation of a feather-light rein aid. Although most of the work is done in the open-air school, summer and winter, a fair portion is undertaken within the larger paddocks or along the paths and rides in the grounds. Naturally enough, the school figures play a major role. However, by way of variation, a time–distance system is used in the grounds, with the minute being used as the time unit.

I had an excellent athletics trainer when I was at university and had ambitions to run the 440 metres and the mile. He used to make me walk twenty-five yards, trot twenty-five yards and run the same distance during the initial passages of training. He demanded a long swinging walk to begin with, followed by a shorter step during which the knee had to be lifted and as well bent as when running. It took several weeks of this kind of exercise before I was allowed to run any distance. As my condition increased, I trotted cross-country, short distances of a couple of miles up to ten miles at a restrained pace somewhat faster than present-day jogging, during which the action of the leg was taken into account, the knee being well bent almost up to the level of the abdomen.

I apply much the same principles when conditioning a horse under a rider. One hundred yards at walk, 100 yards at trot over a period of two weeks soon conditions a soft horse and brings him forward to the addition of 100 yards at canter, on a repetition of the cycle for another two weeks. The heart rate, expressed through the pulse, should be taken. This may be easily done under either side of the jaw by placing the second and third fingers on the submaxillary artery which is located there. The pulse beat is from 30 to 40 beats per minute. Since the object of *all* training is to lower the heartbeat and subdue breathing, under physical stress, the work up to condition must be careful and be taken relatively slowly at first until everything hardens up.

The pulse rate should be taken after the animal has been cantered during early and subsequent training. The rate will be lowered as condition improves; the horse will not blow so hard nor so soon as at first and will sweat less. The perfect example of a horse in top training and condition could be seen in Miss Virginia Holgate's three-day eventer, Priceless, at the 1984 Olympic Games in Los Angeles.

The normal pleasure rider will want his horse to cover country well, though will not necessarily require it to be at a high pitch of training. He will want an animal which is capable of being hunted but not necessarily in hard training to the point that it must have sufficient daily work to keep it so. Enforced idleness for an animal in top training may bring about azoturia, which is a degenerative muscular condition especially over the loins and hindquarters. An animal in top training which is going to be worked less, *should be as carefully slowed down as it has been built up.* Its exercise period should be reduced gradually and its grain feed likewise. This is always a problem where a horse in peak condition is injured and has to be laid up for a while – a definite instance where veterinary advice is required. Azoturia may also overtake a horse that is put back to hard work after an enforced period of rest. Tirade had it once when I was away and her rider overworked her. Fortunately my wife spotted it and called the vet in time. An injection saved the mare.

Every serious working session is begun after the horse has been lightly ridden for ten minutes in order to loosen it up. Five minutes are allotted to riding at walk on a loose rein, about two or three minutes at walk on a long rein and the rest of the time at a collected walk. After that, 110 yards (100 metres) per minute at walk, then 275 yards (250 metres) per minute at trot, followed by 110 yards (100 metres) at walk for one minute. Then come 550 yards (500 metres) at canter for one minute, followed by 110 yards (100 metres) or more at walk back to the school. Then a session of thirty minutes executing the school figures, followed by a pleasant walk with the odd trot, and back to the stable.

Times and distances are increased as the horse shows good condition. As in training a human athlete, walking periods are allowed between strenuous exercises until the 1:1 ratio is changed because of the animal's ability to sustain a longer period at trot or canter. Taking the figure of one to represent the walk, ratios of 1:2 or 1:3 and even 1:4 may be reached as progress allows. How and when the ratios are increased must depend upon the trainer's feeling and observation. Obviously, if the pupil is blown after 1000 yards (1000 metres approx.) at gallop or shows signs of abnormal sweating, the condition is poor and the horse should not be strained. If the pupil is badly blown, then it should be walked on a loose rein and the saddle girth eased. Common sense must prevail and the training plan revised.

Consequently, it may be necessary to return to the start of the training programme by going for long walks in-hand with some light riding at walk and trot until fitness begins to show. All this should have been done before asking anything much of the animal in the first place, and a horse that has been worked in-hand is unlikely to show any form of physical stress. However, if a horse has not been worked at all and has been out at grass, it requires about six weeks of building up to have it fit.

The time:distance ratios I have given are not hard on the horse and are therefore good for building up. They amount to the following speeds of progression per hour: at walk 3¾ miles (6 km) per hour; at trot 9¼ (15 km) per hour; and at canter 18½ miles (30 km) per hour. The ground coverage in yards per minute has already been given above.

Although it really is a matter of each to his own method and competence, I have found my horses in pretty good shape following these conditioning methods. Since I am only concentrating on physical shape here, I do not touch on the disciplines which the young horse must learn from its rider. Those really interested would be well advised to read Mary Rose's book on training,[4] aimed mainly at young professional horse people, and Dr Klimke's *Cavaletti*.[5] Both books will provide all that is needed. The appendix to Dr Klimke's book gives four- to six-week training programmes for animals in their second-year training. These are exceedingly useful. There are three programmes: the first being basic, the second relating to dressage, and the third concerning show-jumpers. While all three are connected with cavaletti work and suggest a day-by-day routine, they are especially interesting to anyone who is concerned with the proper division in time in a training programme and in relation to each particular discipline advocated.

Once the horse has come under the saddle, the whole course of its life is changed, and it will be trained to follow the direction of its own and its rider's special talents. It is growing up. What, during the days of its youth, were the main disciplines, have now become adjuncts and correctives. However, the basic principle should not change and all that has been taught to the horse should be made use of and applied by its rider.

Whatever we do with, or to, our horse, should be governed by our understanding. Riding is not a physical act alone. A good horseman rides primarily with his mind, not merely with his body. At the same time, he knows what he is demanding of his mount and how much it is capable of, as well as what he wishes it to do.

It is somewhat similar in the case of a good handler and trainer. He works primarily with his mind. He knows what he wants to achieve, knows his animal, how far it is mentally capable of learning what he is attempting to teach it. It is his ambition to end with a relatively fearless, totally trusting, gentle and obedient animal; one that is without complexes and is neither a danger to society nor to itself. That is the art of training and handling.

References

1. MÖRMANN, H. and PLÖGER, E., *Buskaschi in Afghanistan*, Verlag C.J. Bucher, Lucerne and Frankfurt, 1978.
2. MACSWINEY OF MASHANAGLASS, THE MARQUIS, *Six Came Flying*, Michael Joseph, London, 1971.
3. CLOWER, M., *Pacemaker International*, London, June 1978.
4. ROSE, MARY, *Training Your Own Horse*, George Harrap & Co. Ltd, London, 1977.
5. KLIMKE, DR.R., *Cavaletti*, J.A. Allen & Co. Ltd, London, 1969.

CHAPTER 5

Flight Orientation and Fear

THOUSAND OF YEARS of domestication have made horses tractable and friendly towards man, accepting him as friend and provider, or allowing themselves to be shamefully enslaved by him, killed in his causes or otherwise abused. The first men to domesticate horses must have been remarkable. We do not know if they penned horses and kept them as a source of meat, or if they set about making use of them as a means of transport, but whichever, they must have understood how to communicate with them and how to make them overcome their natural fears, so inducing an animal that they had hunted, to accept and trust them.

The road from *Eos Hippos* to the modern horse has been a long one. Despite mixtures and selective breeding, the domestic horse as we know it today, retains, in the mass of its heredity, traits and customs that can be found amongst free-living, wild, primitive and feral members of the equine species.

It has become rather the vogue to talk about horses as animals of the steppes and as 'flight oriented'. I grant that this is a romantic concept. Ready flight does apply to wild horses, feral animals and primitives, but with great respect, it can hardly be applied to domestic and domesticated horses. It is, I believe, closer to the truth to describe domestic horses as *fear-reactive animals*, because of their inborn caution, their sensitivity and nervousness. Like their wild and feral cousins, they are readily upset by things which they cannot easily identify and will be frightened when confronted by them. They will remain suspicious and restive, uttering sundry snorts, until they satisfy themselves and know what is going on.

All living things are infused with a modicum of healthy fear of the unknown, *homo sapiens* included. It is right that it should be so because it is nature's self-preservation mechanism that triggers measures calculated to hinder possible injury from attack. Were our domestic horses highly flight sensitive, we should find it impossible to catch them in the paddock, or be able to get anywhere near enough to do so. They would be forever maintaining an 'escape distance', making close approach impossible. An escape distance is a measurable distance which an animal species preserves constantly between itself and an approaching stranger. Most wild things maintain some sort of territorial distance between themselves and potential danger. If this is over-stepped and cannot be preserved, the creature makes off as the stranger comes nearer. The 'escape distance', as it was named by H. Poulson,[1] appears to vary considerably according to habitat, species and expectation of danger from man or other natural enemies. The term is borrowed here and applied to horses, although originally used in relation to the escape distances preserved by various types of swans.

Distances required by swans cited in the works of Poulson and other scientists interested in that species, are quoted by Banko,[2] and, while they do not concern us here, the observation that as birds kept in enclosures gradually become tame, the escape distance also gradually decreases, is worth noting.

It is true that an element of the instinct to preserve an escape distance may be seen when strangers approach domestic horses, or when, having been frightened, they run away for a short distance, then turn and try to identify the cause of their fright. In my opinion, the latter is more due to their bifocal sight than to flight requirement. They simply have to get far enough away, in order to have a good look. It would be wrong to believe that a horse which cannot be caught in its paddock is showing signs of inborn flight orientation; it is simply showing the depth of its bad education or naughtiness.

How far fear is precautionary is borne out by Dr K. Zeeb[3] in his observations of the primitive herd belonging to H.H. the Duke of Croëy on the Merfelder Bruch, Duelmen, Westphalia. Although escape distances are extant there, they are very low indeed, because the animals are accustomed to the proximity and sight of humans. While the herd sentinels, which are mares, will take up position and stand tense and erect when the approaching 'danger' is five hundred metres away, the herd will not take flight if approached quietly; the animals will resume grazing while keeping an eye on the intruder. On a hot summer's day, the herd may be approached to within three yards. This applies only to day and night, not to early morning or at dusk, when the escape distance towards humans is preserved at from six to eight yards and sometimes more. Zeeb believes that this is due to 'hereditary memory', because hunting animals would attack during dusk.

If the human simulates a quadruped, the escape distance will be increased immediately to about twenty or so yards. If the quadruped remains quite still, the horses will come to within six or eight yards, nodding their heads and sniffing the air. Should the quadruped move, then the twenty yards' distance will be re-established. If this simulated 'animal' made a violent movement, the herd would flee and establish a new escape distance from three hundred to four hundred yards between itself and the danger. It is interesting to note that, although the herd had plenty of space at its disposal, the escape distance remained relatively short. The scientist tells us something extraordinary occurred when the 'quadruped' stood up to become a human being again. The animals approached to within the normal escape distance which they preserve towards humans. The conclusion is that they cannot distinguish between a crouched human and an animal. Zeeb's observations agree with those of Vavra that the families within the herd come together during flight and that the stallions follow the herd and are not infected by panic.

One experiment with the Duelmener primitive ponies fascinated me sufficiently to try it out on domestic horses. I lay down in one of our paddocks and also tried to simulate a large animal on all fours. The results were disappointing and funny at the same time. The mares came up to have a look and to find out what I was up to. They stood over me and snuffled at me and stood on guard for a time, as though I might be in need of some sort of help, then wandered off and began to graze. At least I found out that domestic horses show no reaction, other than polite curiosity, to the antics of people whom they know. Fortunately, the people hereabouts are used to such strange behaviour and have long since ceased to regard me as odd. The spectacle of an ageing and shabbily-clad gentleman on all fours within a paddock, surprises neither man nor horse. It should be pointed out, however, that the horses know me and my scent.

Dr Zeeb's studies underline the statement that the tamer the animal, the shorter the escape distance found necessary for minimum caution. We had the same experience with Tufted Duck visitors, which, coming every year to live and breed on the ponds, began a gradual decrease of their initial escape distance of approximately one hundred yards, over a period of five years, and no longer took flight when a human was within ten yards of them. Domestic horses have therefore only a vestigial inclination to flee, and will do so only if put into a state of panic.

It is somewhat different where wild, feral and primitive herds are concerned. Vavra[4] observes that surprise or something unknown will set horse herds into panic-stricken flight, with the highest-rank mares and their foals in the

75

forefront, the subordinate mares and their foals in the middle, and the lead stallions of family groups bringing up the rear and driving stragglers forward. He points out that the stallions do not appear to be affected by the general state of panic. Unfortunately, Vavra does not give us even an approximate distance covered by a herd in flight, from starting to stopping point.

Fear is quite a different matter. One may say that it is skin deep and comes readily to the surface. But fear is common to all animals, including the human being. It is at once an unpleasant sensation, a painful emotion, apprehension of danger, pain or alarm. I have said it should be regarded as a protective mechanism that triggers off an action or a chain of actions, including, under given circumstances, aggression. It is so much part and parcel of the horse's make-up, that instead of laying emphasis on their inclination to flee, I prefer to think of them as fear oriented, although one cannot have the one without some proportion of the other.

Anyone who seriously intends to handle horses, should devote some thought to the subject, thereby saving himself many unpleasant and unexpected surprises. Part of the work involved in the education and training of the horse, and especially in the everyday handling of it, whether at work in the yard or in the stable, is literally to teach it not to be afraid. I spend more time doing this than I spend otherwise, and frequently find myself having to teach young people not to be afraid, in order to prevent them infecting the animals with which they come into contact.

Although I believe fear to be endemic, it must be differently constituted in horses than in man. A horse that is frightened does not stop to examine and assess the source of its fear. Nor does it ask itself why it should be frightened by whatever the cause is. Its fear is seldom anticipatory, but usually reflexive. The cause, real or imagined, is there and the horse is stimulated by it instantly. It does not ask itself 'Need I be afraid?'

So, generally speaking, the answer in dealing with any

unknown entity is not to be found in investigation and discovery, but in getting away from it as fast as those strong legs will carry their owner and then, when a safe distance has been reached, to turn around, head held high, to look and scent the possible danger. And should this danger, whatever it may be, come nearer, the horse will resort to withdrawal once again. If the danger does not follow, the horse will settle down to graze, having obviously put the matter out of its mind.

Fear must always be reckoned with. To my mind there are two varieties to contend with in the domestic horse. There is natural fear, as I call it, which may be equated to the human concept of 'I don't know what it is, it may blow up and I'd better get away a bit and have a look first,' and conditioned fear born of personal experience as, for example, fear of the whip, or only rolling on one side at a time and not rolling over completely because of the memory of having been cast in the box.

The natural fears are non-malignant and can be very easily dealt with, either by going up to the cause and touching it, or going past the object in front of the horse, thereby allaying the fear by example, or by the soothing sound of the voice, which quietens the animal. A good example of what may be done is dismounting and leading the horse through shallow water or big puddles. For some reason or another, domestic horses are very often water-shy, which is a nice way of saying that they are afraid of it. This may be due to the fact that they are incapable of assessing the depth of large puddles which, as far as they are concerned, may be the opening to the bottomless pit. While very large puddles may be avoided by extremely dextrous sidestepping which is almost a pleasure to watch, or if need be, by jumping, the same does not apply to river fords, where the horse which is afraid of water will refuse to go any further. In fact the only way that it might go through would be if it were in blind panic.

This fear of water is not to be found amongst wild, feral or primitive horses, who will go into water voluntarily either to escape insects or to get to the opposite bank, or even to take a bath. It is most probable that going into water is not traditional amongst many domestic horses, by which I mean that they have not learned to do so from the mare or the herd leaders, which, having been reared in domesticity, are probably as fearful and inept as the generation below them. Vavra shows marvellous photographs of horses in water and notes in his text that horses are good natural swimmers, even though they are most vulnerable when in the water. But animals in Andalusia and the Camargue and the primitive horses of the Merfelder Bruch all roll in water or mud (Vavra and Zeeb) and enjoy doing so. It should be remembered that horses' lives and reflexes are affected by local conditions, and that great numbers of domestic horses never come near to, or find the necessity for, crossing any amounts of water. Moreover, horses learn from one another, and if a foal has not learned to go into or cross water at the side of its mother, it will show reluctance even to wet its feet. Such an animal will be positively afraid of water. This fear will be founded on fear of the unknown and possibly upon an inability to assess depth when the head is raised, due to the construction of the equine eye.

To beat, or otherwise force, a water-shy horse would create what I call an induced fear, or, if you prefer, condition a reflex negatively. There must be thousands of horses who have been mishandled and which, as a result of it, suffer from induced fears.

The textbook method of the human showing the way through water by entering it and wading, is the correct one, because in so doing the handler makes up for the gap in education left by the mare who had no opportunity of teaching.

While we may deal very successfully with natural fears by showing the animal that the causes are groundless, providing they are not abstract in their form, conditioned fears are quite another matter. The root causes of these fears are carried in the animal's long memory, and as soon as there is an association of any kind, the horse will immediately put up a defence. I go so far as to say that most horse problems stem from a recollection of fears which have been created by ineptness or inexperience on the part of tutor or owner. The problem is that as soon as a horse has learned to put up a successful defence against something, it will call upon this technique whenever it feels the need to do so.

If we take some obvious examples, we can say that if a horse is beaten about the head with a whip, it will not only fear the sight of all whips in future, but having become shy of its head, it will defend its head whenever anyone tries to touch it. Beat a horse in its box – a cardinal crime in any event – and the horse will defend itself, by whatever means, every time anyone tries to touch it when in its box. Bully a horse in its box and the same thing will happen.

But there are many other ways of conditioning fear, which are occasioned rather by lack of understanding, than because of any deliberate act. A fear can be conditioned by trying to force a horse past something that is suspect to it, instead of getting off its back and going up to the cause and showing that the fear is groundless. A horse may be made afraid of being loaded, by employing any of the forcing techniques that are seen so often; threatening with a broom from behind; slinging a lunge rein above the hocks and trying to force the animal up the ramp by this kind of pressure; or even worse, by giving it a crack with the whip the very moment that it puts its forefeet on the ramp. In doing any of these things, a fear is conditioned, which then becomes conceptual, for the animal memorises the cause and will couple the experience with the event. As soon as it does this, it will also remember the successful defence and resort to it when it is faced with the same situation on some other occasion.

It is wrong to force or punish animals for what appears to be disobedience when, in fact, they are defending themselves against things that excite fear and are therefore exercising their natural sense of self-preservation. Fear can always be overcome by practical demonstration and patience, by making the animal understand the situation. To punish after an event is to invite problems in the future. They are then of your own making. People who do so are guilty in a very high degree of what I am always being accused of, when I talk to horses – they are humanising the animal. What they are actually saying is 'You *know* that you are doing *wrong* and you are being *disobedient* and therefore I will *punish* you for not *obeying*.' Of course, they do not say it in so many words, nor even consciously think that way, but that is their attitude. Thus they will condition a fear that may take years to eradicate.

Each word that I have put in italics implies a concept. Dr Jane Goodall very aptly entitled her book on wild dogs, golden jackals and spotted hyenas, *Innocent Killers*,[5] and in so doing, I believe, made a bigger contribution towards human understanding of animal 'morality', than even she may have realised when deciding on the title. Animals are innocent, totally innocent at all times. Good and evil, obedience and disobedience and, above all, punishment, are concepts beyond a horse's fund of stored knowledge. I repeat that if a tutor sees fear is the reason why his mount stands back, shies or stands stock still, his job is to show *why* there is nothing to fear.

On the other hand, while punishment is not an acceptable concept under any condition, a sharp tap with the jumping stick at the right moment, as an added shock designed to make the horse go forward if it doesn't want to face up to a jump, and therefore shows what is known as disobedience under the saddle, is quite another matter. It is a sharp 'aid', but not a punishment. The horse will respond to it in the heat of the moment and most probably forget it, or if it remembers, go to its work in such a manner that there will be no repetition of the experience.

The height of punishment that I will inflict on any horse in-hand, is a slap on the shoulder with the back of my hand, backed by a word of displeasure. The slap usually hurts me more than the recipient, but it serves to convey the 'no nonsense from you' message. That is usually enough.

What I have written above may appear to contradict what

I am about to say now, that the so-called 'punishment' of a horse which shows unwillingness to do something asked of it, is a most efficient way of inducing fear. The sting of the riding whip is only valid when the horse is being ridden. Remember the effect of forcing and punishing a horse that shows an aversion to being loaded into a trailer. Punished in such a situation, the animal will not only continue to fear what it is forced to overcome, but will come to fear it more, because of the punishment received which it does not understand. It will memorise this, and it is often the root cause of a horse's reluctance to allow itself to be loaded.

Waving a cap or a white handkerchief at a horse in order to make it stand back, will induce fear, so will shouting at it, being rough and sudden with hand movements, slamming the bit into the mouth or slapping the saddle hard down on the back, loss of temper with the horse, threatening it with the pitchfork if it comes too near during mucking out, shooing it off when it comes up to inspect what you are doing in its box.

It is by no means impossible to train a horse to accept unhorsemanlike behaviour and to overcome its fear of it. Police horses are trained to remain calm in the face of all kinds of adversities. I have long trained my horses to ignore waved stable rubbers, to allow themselves to be brushed with a broom, or massaged with a fanshaped leaf rake, as well as to ignore strange things that may be waved at them by strangers. But in every single instance a horse so trained is aware of what is happening and is unsurprised by it. It may be concluded that fear is provoked, not, as one might believe, by the strangeness of the object, nor by whatever element of surprise there may be, although it will contribute to the end effect, but by the unknown.

On the other hand, experiments with shot-guns, which I made some years ago, confirmed that horses may be accustomed to the sound of shots. Two friends showed the horses the guns and went into the neighbouring paddock after doing so, while I remained with the animals. Several shots were fired into the air. I remained leaning and immobile on the paddock rail observing the horses. These had both myself and the guns in their line of vision and were quite close to me. The first salvo made the animals start up and waver slightly, as though undecided whether to put distance between themselves and the scene of the occurrence or not. The second salvo had them looking curiously in the direction of the guns. They had begun to graze by the time that the fifth salvo was fired, and did not even bother to look up.

For the next few days, I made a habit of going out with a gun and firing a shot at a distance of about fifty metres away from them after they had been allowed to inspect the gun. Here the sound was linked with an action that became known to them. The sight of the gun was, and still is, combined with a bang. The factor is known. One other interesting thing was that my indifference during the firing of the initial shot, the normality of my voice, and my relaxed attitude at the fence during the firing of the subsequent salvos, probably gave them the assurance that the sound of a shot represented no danger to themselves, because their 'herd leader' did not react to the shots.

The second example is connected with a blue plastic garbage disposal bag, which was left in the stable yard near the garbage bins put out there once a week for the refuse collectors. This bag was placed beside the bins when Tirade was out in the paddock. I was bringing her in when she spotted it from a distance of about sixty-five yards, and became unbelievably agitated, snorting, dancing and swinging on her lead rein, arching her neck, dilating her nostrils and pricking her ears. I did not see the cause of the excitement and marched forward. When I did see the bag, I lengthened the rein as much as I could, walked up to the sack and began to stroke it and talk to it. Tirade was a filly at the time, very nervous and skittery, but also more than ordinarily inquisitive. She remained standing at the end of the rein for a little while, then, as she became certain that all was clear, came slowly up and inspected the bag herself. Adonis, the dressage horse which I have already mentioned, behaved in exactly the same way in relation to a black plastic bag left close to his box door. He responded to the same treatment in the same manner. Both occurrences led to a number of experiments by the placing of various objects at different points in the yard, although not simultaneously. I discovered that the way the light struck the shiny surface of a bag affected the reaction to it. The same bag carried in or out of a box was regarded with comparatively little interest. It, or any object, only assumed importance when it was placed where the horses would normally expect to find nothing.

The range of fear stimuli is very large and cannot be pinpointed. Let me give examples. Tirade was excited by the slapping of broad rhododendron leaves in the wind and, had she not been in-hand, would have run away. As it is impossible to 'explain' sound in visual terms, it was equally impossible to introduce her to the source and thereby lay the cause of the fear. The only method was to use the 'courage' of a lead stallion – in this case that of the handler – and his confidence and calm in the face of the supposed danger. In this instance the source of fear may be described as abstract, since the actual sound and the reason for it, the slapping leaves, could not be action-linked and so associated and assimilated by the brain of the animal. It was clearly evident that the mare associated the sound with the presence of some hostile thing within the big bush, and not with the rhododendron itself.

Anything that is not normally in a particular place will cause fear and shying away. Piles of sticks and of fallen branches stacked along familiar rides in woods or through coppices, will cause anxiety and lead to abnormal behaviour. Horses should not be ridden past, unless absolutely necessary, but shown the offending thing as harmless, should there be time to do so. If this is done, the animal, as it gets older, will tend to regard most strange objects as harmless.

Motor cars and tractors or delivery vans are as much accepted as bicycles, but the parking of a large Mercedes with an even larger horse trailer, sent the pony filly, Leila, into something near to a frenzy, although she had been loaded into such a trailer without effort when she first came to us. My talking to the trailer and a great deal of stroking it, gave her enough self assurance to come close to it and to examine it herself. Constant examination of fear-exciting factors will eventually make the horse steady in the face of outside influences, and a young or new horse that has been subjected to 'orientation' walks, as described in a later chapter, can be brought to the point where fears may be allayed by the quiet use of the voice, without necessarily having to examine the cause of the fear. The spoken words, 'steady' or 'it's all right', should then be sufficient to help it overcome real or imagined fears.

While almost all the natural fears may be comparatively easily dealt with through sensible handling, induced fears, as I call them, present problems, especially in the case of older horses that one has not educated oneself from the very start. Our understanding of the natural fears helps us to avoid making mistakes that will condition induced ones.

I had a gelding named Favorit with me for a time, and he had what we Irish call 'a great jump in him', which he would use to clear the paddock rails anytime that police-car and fire-engine sirens frightened him as they passed by on the public road. This might have been a bad thing if he had not invariably made for the safety of his own box, where he would remain peaceably until found. This got me into the habit, incidentally, of always leaving stable and box doors wide open when horses are out in the paddock. Should anything happen that might frighten them and they break out, likely as not they will seek the safety of their own home, if they are well treated there.

Once fear has been aroused, it is better for humans to remain calm. There is no point in flapping about and chasing the horse. You should behave normally in order not to create the atmosphere afresh. The best thing to do is to first close all gates that might allow the animal to get off the property, find a carrot and a piece of newspaper, and then set off quietly with a lead rein in your pocket, intent on catching up the escapee. The horse has usually forgotten the source of its fear by the time these things have been done and will be grazing quietly – usually somewhere you don't want hoof marks. Because it is a well-educated horse and knows you, it will come to find out if the rustling paper in the hand really does have something pleasant wrapped in it. The answer is the carrot, so the next time that the horse breaks out it is not going to hesitate for too long before approaching.

There is a world of difference between a horse that takes fright and breaks out of its own accord, and one that is quite deliberately frightened and put to flight. The first will calm down relatively quickly if left alone to do so; the other may have to be gone after, because it is no longer within the confines of the property; the usual measures cannot be taken and the animal has become a public menace.

I believe that if one wishes to deal with fear effectively we must consider the horse's vision and nervous system and calculate on that basis. It is relatively simple to teach yourself to see and think like a horse, which in this context means to more or less accurately predict and calculate how a horse is liable to react, before it does so.

The handler's vision is quite different to his charge's. It is wrong to imagine, as is so often heard said, that horses have 'poor' sight. What they have is a different and more specialised form, fitting to their nature and their way of life.

How good is a horse's vision, and how far does its difference to human vision affect its behaviour?

Smythe and Goody[6] provide us with detailed explanations of the construction and functioning process of the equine eye, which may help us to understand the pictures entering a horse's brain and the possible reaction to them.

The horse is not possessed of central vision. It does not concentrate its vision on an object that is ahead. With the eyes placed somewhat laterally, each eye sees a different picture simultaneously. This means that if you are standing on the left side, the animal will see you with that eye, while seeing whatever is happening on its right side at the same time, as well as what is ahead and behind it: ideal equipment for a creature that will protect itself by moving away.

Due to the particular construction of the eyeball, where the lower part is more flattened than the upper, and the arrangement of the retina on a slope, the horse is able to focus on near and far objects at the same time. Because the lens is not elastic, as is the case in the human eye, the animal is forced to raise and lower its head if it wants to make an image clear. In doing so, it will bring the image onto the part of the retina that will bring the object being observed to the right distance. A horse that is concentrating will raise its head and prick its ears.

Smythe and Goody tell us that the horse will see no object lying in front of it quite clearly, if the distance does not exceed four feet.

It is within the realms of possibility that vision plays an appreciable part in influencing the flight and fear of these creatures. Yet whilst their capability to see so many varying pictures in front and from the side and back must contribute to their safety in incidents representing real danger, and allow them to feed and watch what is going on around them at the same time, it must force them, or so one would believe, to put some distance between themselves and anything that may arouse their fear, not only to avoid it, but to allow them to assess it.

It should be remembered that horses are extremely sensitive, nervous and easily upset. They miss very little of what is going on about them, combining their sharp sense of smell and their eyesight to keep themselves well informed. Yearlings and foals are scared by most things that they are unfamiliar with, not least sudden or strange movements of things with which they are already familiar. The unexpected closing of a stable door immediately beside the hitching rail to which the filly Leila was tethered, so scared the animal that it tried to stand on its hind legs, and only my quick release of the 'panic' catch prevented her from falling over. Once released, she made off a few yards across the yard and began to look for something to eat. When I caught her up, it would have been hard to believe that anything had frightened her less than half a minute earlier.

Little incidents of a like nature are quite normal with youngsters that have not yet learned the facts of life and are mostly caused by tight-strung nerves. At their age especially, excessive noise, shouting, bullying or thoughtless behaviour will cause positive damage to the nervous system, as will demands that overtax the mental and physical capacity.

We used to visit Tirade when she was recovering from a serious operation following a nasty accident involving runaway mares. A beautiful mare occupied the neighbouring box, and her state of lethargy and depth of depression gave the impression that she must be seriously ill, although she was without any visible mark. I asked the veterinary surgeon who owned the clinic and was treating both horses, what was wrong with her, and he told me that she was a three-year-old suffering from a bad nervous breakdown.

The mare was highly talented and more than ordinarily willing. She was already competing in jumping competitions and had won a number of them. Her owners, proud of their phenomenal young horse, were ambitious and did not spare her. Obviously the excitement of the jumping arena, constant travel and change of scene, plus the psychological pressure, had proved to be too great a strain on her nervous system. She became depressed. The vet hoped that he might get her right again, but it would take time. The lack-lustre look and the total lack of interest in anything, showed clearly in the dull, sad eyes; and the way she turned away her elegant head when spoken to said only too clearly how much she wanted to be left alone. The whole being of the animal contrasted so sharply with the keen alertness of Tirade who, despite her dreadful injury, was all eagerness and full of life.

The young animal had been brought forward too fast at too young an age. Had she been mine, at this age she would just about have been learning to accept the feel of saddle and girth for the first time; she would never have been rushed into such an early career.

I shall, however, be discussing the 'spiritual' aspect of horses later on, so that I will not make any further comment here.

References

1. POULSON, H., *Dansk Ornithologisk Fornings Tidesskrift*, Vol.42, No.4, 1949.
2. BANKO, WINSTON, *The Trumpeter Swan*, No.63, The United States Department of the Interior.
3. ZEEB, DR K., *Wildpferde in Dülmen*, 4th edition, Hallwag Verlag, Bern and Stuttgart, 1974.
4. VAVRA, R., *Pferdestudien*, Co-Libris Verlagsgesellschaft, Munich, 1979.
5. LAWICK and GOODALL, *Innocent Killers*, Collins, London, 1970.
6. SMYTHE, R. H. and GOODY, P.C., *The Horse*, J.A. Allen & Co. Ltd, London, 1973.

CHAPTER 6

Perception and Communication

IT IS HIGHLY PROBABLE that animals are equipped with a very high degree of sensory and extrasensory perception (ESP) about which we know little or nothing, but with which we come into daily contact in our work with them. If we are not prepared to accept such a probability then it becomes increasingly difficult to explain certain behaviour that is neither reflexive nor attributable to instinct. How, for example, does my mare apparently *know* when I am driving our car, and greet it vocally and with head nodding when it is out of her sight, but does not do so when it is driven by my wife? I am told by my wife that this is the case.

The same sort of behaviour was observed on the part of my Labrador retriever, Tatja, on days when I was returning from longer absences, sometimes from journeys abroad. She would become restless all day and take up waiting positions hours before I was within sight or sound range, and her restlessness would increase the nearer I came to home. How did the dog know, or how does the horse know?

This puzzling question allows room for speculation when trying to come up with an answer, for I certainly do not believe that such manifestations are unique to either *my* horse or *my* dog. Far rather do I believe that they occur frequently elsewhere, but may pass unnoticed or, if noticed, be thought unique to the animal concerned. Nor can it be that they are directly connected with reflexes, instincts or learning; far more likely with purely hereditary traits.

Herd observation, domestic, feral or wild, does not seem to disclose anything of this nature that would allow us to reach a reasonable conclusion as to precise sources. One can only *presume* that such ability is developed by the circumstances which determine the manner in which individual horses live. Most animal species have to subject their needs, as well as their behaviour pattern, to the situation in which they find themselves, although original social behaviours, like dominance and rank, remain basically the same and continue in the behaviour of breeds which have been domesticated for centuries, or breeds that have been evolved from a combination of such breeds.

Horses, as we see them at any show, are seldom 'pure'. They are mostly mixtures. This would even appear to apply to the thoroughbred's origin, for there is uncertainty concerning the origins of the foundation mares, a subject that is expertly covered by Roger Longrigg.[1] It is possible that the only pure horse is the Arabian or Eastern horse, or the truly wild ones.

Each mixture of blood must also carry with it some of the habitual and genetic characteristics of the breeds concerned, which, in turn, must ultimately affect the character and the habits of the individuals produced from such unions. Naturally, race mixtures which eventually breed true are 'pure' of their kind and are recognised as such. Breeds are mixed for various reasons – the thoroughbred came into being through the efforts of breeders to produce a better 'running horse' – but are mostly purpose-oriented, in that there is hope that the offspring will show the positive characteristics of sire and dam. Thus, one hopes to improve the quality of the product by introducing thoroughbred or Arabian entires to native mares, not only by passing on physical characteristics but spiritual ones as well. According to Wynmalen, one infusion of Arabian blood suffices to outbreed all sorts of native unsoundness and defect. Moreover, it will pass on soundness of wind, sight and strength of bone as well as its intelligence and gentle temperament.

Although we have no idea of what goes on in the equine mind, many of us are quite happy to assume that nothing much goes on in there. Careful day-to-day observation allows us to recognise activities that are directly attributable to reflexes or, if one prefers, to wholly natural urges. The animal species is non-aggressive as a whole and mainly concerned with the problems of self-nourishment and social status *inter se*. Problems do arise when two animals with dominant characters, while desiring each other's company, nonetheless behave aggressively towards their partner, or partners, and will attempt to take the leading position at intervals during the day. I have this difficulty with my Arabian mare and the half-bred Arabian who shares her life. Regrettably, both animals show scars of repeated kickings, but were I to keep them apart the problems of management would be even greater. This rivalry increases in my presence, or when both are in season, when the incidence of aggressive displays and kickings increases. The only true solution would be to dispose of one or the other.

A horse will live very peaceably if allowed to do so and it is really the matter of rank and sexual drive which are the main causes of disagreements between members of a domestic herd and its groupings. Left to its own devices and allowed to live as it pleases, a horse will neither try to broaden its horizon nor feel the need to do so.

Close association with the human animal alters this situation. The horse is no longer left to develop in its own way. Instead, demands are made upon it and its living rhythm is disturbed and regulated. Not only that, but coming from one social order, it is demanded of it that it fit into another, with all that that implies. The domestic horse must learn to fit into two societies and accept the rules of both. Not even dogs, whom we rate very highly, are asked to do this to the same extent.

We know nothing about the role played by telepathy between animals generally, but it is not outside reasonable speculation that such communication exists, and its existence would account for quite a number of things. Communication of mind and mind other than through the *known* channels of the senses cannot be ruled out, the more so because modern science knows a great deal more about electromagnetism than it did heretofore.

It is comfortable to attribute the inexplicable in animal reaction to 'instinct' or purely to reflex. When it comes to it, we know little enough about animal instinct, and my dictionary defines it in relation to animals as 'the natural impulse by which they are guided *apparently* independently of reason or experience'. The italics are mine. One should not rule out the possibility that animals can communicate with each other through the disturbance of the normal electromagnetic fields in which they move, so that a change in the heartbeat of an individual, or changes of frequencies of brain impulses due to perceived potential danger may well be picked up, even at some distance, by other members of a herd or group. The realisation that something is amiss or different occurs in the case of dogs. I have experienced that one of our dogs will show signs of aggression towards a stranger who is afraid of dogs generally, picking up the fear signals as far away as fifty metres while standing upwind from the person concerned. Asked if the person is really afraid of dogs, the answer is inevitably positive although there were no visible signs of fear over the distance.

If we examine this a little bit further, we can take as an example the horse that is being led. Complete contact exists between it and the person who is leading. This contact is not only spiritual but also physical, since the lead rein is 'attached' to both parties and therefore acts rather like an electric flex. The same situation exists when the animal is being ridden where the contact is increased not only by the reins but also by the straddling of the animal by its rider. It is the will of the rider, or the person who is leading the horse, and not the power of the aids or the lead rein alone, that controls the animal.

We can accept the fact that each living being is surrounded by an aura, and there is no reason why we should not do so since some sort of aura has been photographed by means of what is known as the 'Kirlian effect', which is in fact electrophotography under special conditions. Certainly the human cell is seen by Soviet scientists as an emitter of electromagnetic radiation, and more – Playfair and Hill[2]. Hill was present during an experiment conducted by the Soviet scientist Inyushin, in which was demonstrated the apparent transfer of energy from one living system to another.

It is therefore conceivable that when the auras of two living beings touch, a reaction in the form of communication may follow. Indeed, if we wish to carry this idea a stage further, what is so impossible about the thought that bad temper may communicate itself in the form of a violent and therefore disrupting electrical 'storm' that upsets the emanation of the other being to the point of causing panic or acute distress? There seems to be little other reason as to why animals pick up atmospheres of irritation, fear or unspoken bad humour and react to them, sometimes to the point of even violent action. Or that they understand and pick up confidence and calm by the same means.

It is beyond any question, whatever the reason, that emanations of human fear, unease, mistrust or good humour, are quickly picked up and reacted upon. A horse that is being led by somebody who is either afraid of it or in a bad humour, is far more difficult to deal with than one which is being handled in a calm and assured manner. I know from experience that if Tirade becomes excited, she may be quickly calmed by the sound of the voice and by placing a hand flat on her shoulder. There are times when her reaction to this is immediate. It somewhat depends upon the degree of excitement, a factor which is, of course, not measurable, at least by everyday means.

However, the calming effect is probably due to the steady

voice backed by an equally steady pulsing of heart and brainwaves which she may well be able to pick up. This is a hypothesis based on the knowledge that all living beings exist in a highly complex electromagnetic world, concerning which not everything is known. Indeed, most of us are quite oblivious of the electromagnetic fields, high and low frequency waves and impulses which we cannot see or properly feel and therefore do not concern ourselves with. There is no justifiable reason to disbelieve that animals might be equipped with a special sensitivity of their own that would allow them to pick up each other's, and our own, brain and heart signals, whatever their frequencies, and convert the impulses of such emissions into a 'language' of communication signals.

If we allow ourselves to speculate further and to play with the concept of such possible communication, we may reasonably imagine that mass panic infection in a herd may be due to a heightening of brain and heart impulses of one or more of the herd's members, electrically picked up by the mass and translated into action – a kind of built-in radio system, with the individual either acting as transmitter or receiver. The idea is not to be taken too lightly or summarily dismissed.

This theory may not be far fetched when we consider the spread of panic in a human herd and how quickly a mass of people so infected may get out of control. Rationalisation of the situation, possible by reason of 'superior' human intelligence, appears to break down, very much as it seems to do amongst panic-stricken animals. I have not yet come across a reasonable explanation as to why this should be so, and the inner trigger releasing unease or panic is not clear.

There is so much that we know nothing about and can only speculate on. Only a few decades ago, none of us were aware of the bat's personal 'radar' or 'sonar' system.

We know that equine herds post sentries, mostly old and experienced mares, especially during those times when the herd is sleeping, as is the case on the Merfelder Bruch, where, outside the breeding season, the herd runs without a stallion. It is different in the case of herds with stallions. Vavra[3] tells us that if he happened to surprise a mare who was some distance from her herd, she would normally stand still during the moment of translation to alarm readiness, and that this would be noticed almost immediately by the herd stallion who would take up the same position, but warn the herd by blowing.

Both mares and stallions show the same reaction, as does a domestic horse when potential danger approaches. Tension, curiosity, the head raised and the ears pricked are the signs.

Unfortunately, Vavra does not reveal what factor triggered the stallion's awareness after the mare assumed her alert position. Granted he may have been watching his mare, or scented the alien being, or even heard him, but the words 'almost immediately' suggest a time lapse not bridged by a vocal warning such as the stallion then gave to the herd by his blowing. It is not outside the realms of possibility that the entire may have picked up an alien vibration that caused him to sense the mare's situation.

So-called sensing of danger may well mean nothing more than picking up alien or disturbed frequencies, or what might be described as abnormal ones which, in some cases, when coupled with scent, sight or hearing, warn of an impending change in the status quo. It need not necessarily mean that the danger is 'active'. Even humans will say that they have a feeling that 'something dreadful is going to happen', which may be due to much the same sets of causes, although we, by reason of our traditional mode of society, may no longer be able to interpret such messages accurately, if at all, because our sensitivities have been blunted to the point of becoming no more than a vague sense of awareness.

We know that this is not the case where animals are concerned and that they are capable of picking up signals of impending catastrophies, becoming restless or excited or showing signs of abnormal behaviour[4] long before an event occurs. There is the case of the Freiburger duck, whose early warning of an impending air-raid, during World War II, was responsible for the saving of countless lives in that city, although she herself perished in the same raid. The grateful citizens erected a monument to her memory, which may be seen to this day.[2]

There is unquestionably a great amount of work to be done in this area before we can dismiss such theories or, for that matter, make dogmatic statements concerning animals, their motivation and their behaviour. Nobody living in this century, with its rapid advances in the natural sciences, should be willing to make pronouncements one way or the other, before the theory has been studied and proved right or wrong. Some of my own experiences with animals tend to make me believe that a good deal of extrasensory perception may explain some of those things that appear to be inexplicable, or that we simplify by putting down to mere 'instinct'.

It does no harm, and may even do a deal of good, to experiment with thought transference when dealing with your own horse, even if it is mere thought and not articulated, for it is highly improbable that the horse can pick up a message in terms of 'word' thoughts or their possible meaning, but it does appear to be able to sense what may well be a change of thought frequency, or, differently expressed, a change of rhythm.

Some experiments in what may best be described as personal relations proved to be quite revealing. It is always said that one should not make a pet of a horse, and I cannot dispute the rightness or wrongness of this, especially as I do not go out from this particular standpoint. The attitude that I believe in, is the one of the herd leader, so I think of myself as a horse, rather than a human, and try to think as they do. Dominance is a continuous intellectual process, not a physical one. In order to dominate in this manner, we must regulate the human side of affairs and not react wholly as a human might. Since we do not belong to the species, we must take the trouble to understand it through observation and then draw logical conclusions. One of the prime concepts is that of giving and receiving trust. If you utterly trust an animal, it will trust you because the feeling is conveyed somehow, most probably, but not provably, by the pattern of your electrical emanations.

There is nothing to dispute that the vibrations of the handler are conducted along the length of the rein. I know from experience just how wrong things can go if I am nervous or irritable or excited by something that may have nothing in common with the animal. I recall an occasion after Tirade had been in a competition, when, irritated and in a hurry, I brought her out of the box in which she had been put for a while, in order that Monika should hack her home.

The mare suddenly went wild and completely out of control. I, who can normally manage her with the bat of an eye and a twitch of a finger, found myself unable to quieten her down. She raced around me at a gallop and refused to listen to my voice which must have held a note of irritation. Fortunately, Herr Bielefeld, who had owned her before I bought her, was standing talking to somebody and I asked him to take her. She was immediately quiet. I had simply transferred my irritation to the animal, and a fair portion of nervousness as well.

I have often found that horse and rider will not get on well together, especially if the rider is off colour or in a bad mood. Monika would have off-days when riding the mare during which nothing would go right. I used to make her ride the animal on the lungeing circle and do gymnastics in the saddle while making fun of her and getting her to laugh. About ten minutes of strenuous work and suppling exercise, plus some fun and the recovery of her sense of humour, had the effect of relaxing the rider, and this was clearly seen in the team as soon as serious work was resumed. The American expression 'up tight' is an apt one when applied to a tense rider on a sensitive horse, the latter becoming as 'tight' as the person upon its back. I am sure that such tensions and their transference from rider to horse, or from horse to rider, account quite frequently for disappointing performances in the jumping ring or dressage arena.

Without going too deeply into the matter, living bodies

emit a variety of electrical signals, and the human body is a source of infra-red radiation. Heart, brain and muscles produce electrical impulses, with those from the brain being ten times weaker than those emitted by the heart. When in an active, thinking state, the brain puts out a beta brainwave of from 14 to 30 Hz, but this by no means represents all of the brain's rhythms. Muscle waves have a frequency of up to 100 kilocycles, or even more. According to the authors Playfair and Hill[2], the various signals co-relate with certain definite mental and physical states.

It does not seem to me to be far-fetched to suggest that with considerable outputs of high- and low-frequency signals being constantly emitted by a human, the animal is likely to pick up correct messages from them, and that these will either agree or disagree with the impulses that it emits itself. If we consider this as a possibility, it might be an acceptable thesis to propose that excited impulses emitted by the human might possibly come into conflict with calm impulses from the horse and agitate them, so producing a kind of electrical storm with negative results.

I do not believe that we know anything about the role played by thermal radiation between horse and rider. It is known that any surface warmer than its surroundings gives off thermal radiation. It is just possible that radiation from the horse and radiation from the rider, intermixed, will promote a certain closeness that creates a special kind of intimate contact. It has always been said that love comes through contact, and I am sure that this is far from wrong. I can see no reason why something similar should not take place between two living beings, even if they are not of the same species. It could be that where the electrical impulses emitted and body radiation of both parties do not mix, the results may be fully negative.

Certainly concentration, or lack of it, on the part of the handler greatly influences the horse, and this would point to a reasonable degree of verity when considering the positive or negative effects of brain and heart-beat frequencies. It would be interesting to follow the theory providing that one had the equipment and the training to read results correctly. But whether capable of proving it scientifically or not, I am convinced that these electrical and magnetic impulses play a far greater role than any of us suspect in relationships with other living beings.

In order to test my own theories, I have attempted, and even succeeded, to make a horse move over by extending a hand to within a few centimetres of its skin, but I have not been able to convince myself that the resultant moving was due to an electrical signal or to the fact that the animal could see me stretch out my hand in a movement that is familiar to it. I have, however, with certainty, been able to calm down rising excitement by holding my hand about two inches away from the horse's skin and telling it to be calm. There are days when the horses literally crackle with electricity and it is possible to draw hairs of the mane towards me by coming near, but not touching, them. But once again, I cannot be sure that the surface of the horse is not charged with static electricity, rather than with emissions of electricity from 'inside'; in other words, a purely atmospheric condition, rather than an emissive one.

Before closing this unfinished theme, mention should be made of 'mood transference'. I take the term directly from Professor Konrad Lorenz,[5] who uses it in discussing the fast-working news system within a pack of rats. If we evaluate some of the points and examples given in this chapter, we may not be too far out if we believe that a somewhat similar news system exists between horses, or between man and horse, whatever the actual communicative base may be. We might even assume telepathy. The day will probably come when we will know about these things with certainty and will be able to make use of the knowledge gained.

In a sense, every book on equitation, and indeed this book on handling, attempts to pass on traditional methods and new ideas arising from personal experience, and so help the rider or handler, and, incidentally, the horse as well.

This is all well and good, but even the most meticulous

application of theory (because it is that until it becomes one's own experience) will not achieve the ultimate result, for the good and excellent reason that we are constantly dealing with imponderables, as well as with the human and equine factor. No two human beings are alike, no two horses may be expected to react alike and no two situations are similar.

Handler, rider and horse are influenced by the condition of their nervous systems at any given moment. It is this that makes the picture an ever-changing one, each being involuntarily picking up vibrations from the other. These may change from moment to moment as the emitted impulses become excited or relaxed. Knowledge of this possibility has been responsible for phrases like 'feeling one's way into the horse' or 'communicating through reins or saddle', which I have strewn liberally through the text of this book.

Horses are possessed of a nervous system that makes them sensitive to a high degree, so that it would be unrealistic to believe that they are merely animals and therefore incapable of distinguishing good from bad humour. But, as I have said elsewhere, the concept of good and bad is an abstract one, which seduces one to believe that when a person is in a bad humour, what the animal feels is a minor electric storm that is unpleasant to it, is picked up and disturbs its own nervous equilibrium.

If, as I suggest, nervous stimuli and electrical impulses and frequencies within the systems of man and animal affect each other through an interplay, then mere technique in handling is not enough. There must be more to the relationship between horse and rider or handler, and this to my mind is communication. I will not deny that supreme technicians of the calibre of Dr Reiner Klimke, Nelson Pessoa, Elizabeth Edgar, William Steinkraus *et al*, could sit in a saddle and get the best out of an indifferent horse. They might, if taxed, even protest that they do no more than get up on its back and produce a fine result by reason of their technical ability alone, by the sureness of their routine in the saddle, but I would argue this. I would believe that their mastery is such that they automatically feel their way into the individual, even if doing so unconsciously. The response that they will get stems from their mastery and the animal's perception of it, passed on by their concentration on their mount; not merely by the technical means that they use to achieve the result.

It is well known that after those competitions where riders are obliged to change over to the horse of another, none of the horses are quite the same for a few days following the experience, although the expertise of the riders concerned cannot be questioned. And it is equally well known that during some of these events, certain horses will put up defences against the strange rider. This is probably due to the fact that the communication is wrong, although the technique is right.

It is a no less remarkable fact, that most of the top riders are remembered by their association with a particular horse. Marion Coakes and Stroller, Colonel Llewellyn and Foxhunter, Nelson Pessoa and Gran Geste, Reiner Klimke and Alerich, to name but a few. One might be inclined to believe that it was horsemanship alone, coupled with high breeding of the animal, that made for success, but a horse named Late Night Final, later renamed Finality, the daughter of a milk-float mare, and her rider, Pat Smythe (now Koechlin-Smythe), tend to upset such a theory. For it was not the development of the horse, Finality, that is alone interesting, nor her origin, but the events that occurred after her sale by her main owner Mr Traill. The horse was sold to Tommy Makins, who, according to Dorian Williams,[6] was one of the greatest names in show jumping in the north of England. The same source tells us that Finality did not go well for him and was sold to a Mr Snodgrass in Scotland, where she did no better. Mr Snodgrass showed wisdom and asked Pat Smythe to ride the mare in the first Horse of the Year Show, 1949. There the pair won the Leading Jumper of the Year Class, although not having been together for very long. To round off the picture, the same lady generously loaned another horse, Prince Hal, as a potential Olympic horse, at a time when women were not allowed to ride in Olympic events. No member of the team could get on with him. The horse was to be given back to its owner at a big show, where the Olympic team was having a public work-out. Although Pat Smythe was not entered for the main event, she asked for permission to jump the horse. Permission granted, she won the event, beating all the Olympic riders, in spite of the fact that she had not ridden the horse for many weeks.

I believe that communication between Pat Smythe and her horses was as near perfect as one could hope for. Stated simply, she knew what to say to them and they knew what she was asking. I do not know what form this communication took, but it must certainly have been based on perfect harmony and a contact that could be expressed in some way through the reins and the saddle, with the vibrations of the two living beings perfectly attuned.

A direct parallel had to, and still must, exist between Hans Gunter Winkler and his horses. There is the almost legendary passage over the parcours during the 1956 Olympics in Stockholm when, sorely injured, he took the celebrated mare, Halla, to victory with a clear round that ensured the gold medal for Germany. This he achieved, despite being injured to the point of incapacity and having to be carried out in order to be put up in the saddle.

There are all sorts of theories concerning this famous ride: that Halla, *knowing* what was at stake, carried her rider over the difficult course or that, according to Horst Stern,[7] who sets out to prove his argument with a series of photographs, superb routine and self-discipline prevailed. I agree with Stern on the evidence of his published pictures, but go a little further in that I believe that the communication between horse and rider was such as to bridge any small deficiencies that may have occurred. It has to be remembered that Halla was a particularly difficult horse. She had failed to allow herself to be ridden until Winkler came along. That it was she who brought him, and he who brought her, to the pinnacle of success, was no mere chance.

Much as I love horses and believe that I understand them and their requirements, much as I believe in their intelligence and their ability to think conceptually to a limited extent, I consider it sheer anthropomorphicism to believe that any horse knows what is at stake when it is in competition. But I do know from experience, and I have touched on the subject throughout this book, that the dominant will and influence of a closely accepted man, will influence the animal all of the way in any particular direction; itself an extraordinary thing.

There is the interesting story of Golden Cygnet, by Deep Run out of Golden Cygneture, one of the best National Hunt horses since Arkle. His last race at Ayr, on April 15th, 1978, put an end to his promising career when contesting his thirteenth race. He had fractured a neck vertebra and made 'mincemeat' of the end of another. However, I am not here concerned with the causes of his death. What I am interested in is the relationship that existed between the trainer, Eddie O'Grady, and Golden Cygnet himself after the accident at the last flight at Ayr.

The horse was not only difficult to break from the start, but also had the nasty habit of putting his head down between his legs when galloping, which made him exceedingly difficult to sit on and resulted in the unseating of many of his riders because he would buck. According to Mr O'Grady, he only succeeded with him 'because of the ability of some of my very good lads'. Even so, he would damage his knee with his teeth when galloping, a habit cured by the introduction of a specially made knee boot. Half an hour after the final race of the Ayr meeting, O'Grady visited the horse, who had appeared to suffer little ill-effect beyond stiffness after his fall, to discover that he had a tremendous swelling on either side of his neck, some four inches behind the poll and another on the lower third of his jugular furrow.

'What happened then was quite uncanny. I stood in the stable with him and he walked up to me and rubbed me with the left side of his head. He took three steps back and then came up to me again and rubbed me with the right side of his head. He went on doing that, up and down, for twenty minutes. It was as if he was trying to say to me "Look, there's something wrong, Look after me, please." It was then that I got on to Edinburgh University.'

Later, O'Grady described Golden Cygnet's 'uncanniness' once again. 'Early on in a race he would relax completely. It was as if the horse knew exactly what racing was all about and exactly when he had to go. Two flights from home he would suddenly take hold of the bit and it was only then that he would start pulling.'

Michael Clower, author of the article from which I have quoted above, was struck by O'Grady's use of the word 'uncanny' on several occasions when talking about Golden Cygnet's behaviour both at home and on the racecourse.[8]

With great respect to Mr O'Grady, I cannot find Golden Cygnet's behaviour 'uncanny', but rather an accolade to him and his lads. O'Grady was obviously the centre of the animal's life, and the relationship pretty near perfect. I know from personal experience that animals come to you at once when they require help. On one occasion, Tirade was almost killed by the mistake of a strange vet, her own one being away at the time. The mare came to me, laid her head in my hands and nudged me gently as though asking help and comfort. And when she finally went down on the straw, she did the same when I bent down to comfort her during what I believed to be her last hours. This went on for five dreadful days until we discovered what was wrong.

I have also experienced something similar with swans that have been injured and that I have treated. Although feral, they would come into one of the yards and wait until I came, allowing me to pick them up without any form of resistance, after which they would submit themselves to treatment which, on one occasion, included a trip in a car and subsequent X-ray at the local hospital.[9] Animals with good experience of humans do know where to turn. An empathy exists, and it is this that they understand.

What one has to work on from the start is the establishment of the relationship.

References

1. LONGRIGG, R., *The History of Horse Racing*, Stein and Day, New York, 1972.
2. PLAYFAIR, G.L. and HILL, S., *The Cycles of Heaven*, Pan Books, London and Sydney, 1979.
3. VAVRA, R., *Pferdestudien*, Co-Libris, Verlagsgesellschaft, Munich, 1979.
4. CANBY, T.V., *National Geographic Magazine*, Vol. 149, No 46, June 1976.
5. LORENZ, Prof. Dr. K., *On Aggression*, Bantam Matrix Editions, 1969.
6. WILLIAMS, DORIAN, *Show Jumping*, Pelham Books, London, 1970.
7. STERN, HORST, *Bemrkungen über Pferde*, Kindler Verlag, Munich, 1973.
8. CLOWER, MICHAEL, *Pacemaker International*, London, June, 1978.
9. MACSWINEY OF MASHANAGLASS, THE MARQUIS, *Six Came Flying*, Michael Joseph, London, 1971.

PART TWO

CHAPTER 7

Education

THE SUCCESSFUL EDUCATION of all animals depends upon
mutual respect and trust. The same applies to later training
and, in the case of a horse, fitting out for its ultimate
purpose. I make the distinction between training and
education in order to separate the two phases involved in
getting the horse ready for its life's work. Education is
primarily the teaching of those manners which the horse
needs in order to live reasonably happily amongst people.
In educating the horse, we deliberately teach it obedience,
which is necessary for safety, especially since the horse is
infinitely stronger than we are. Training is somewhat
different in that we get the animal into physical shape and
teach it those things, for example, the so-called 'aids', which
will open up its future as a riding horse. Both phases have
the same objective: the production of what the late Henry
Wynmalen[1] described as 'the pleasant riding horse'.

Since we are only concerned with work on foot and with
general manners, I will go no further than preparing the
horse for the attentions of the rider who will ultimately take
it on to greater things. And while I am primarily concerned

with green horses, it should be said here that the same principles of education may be readily and successfully used on horses that have been spoiled or those that have no manners at all, even if they are adult and approaching old age.

Foals, like puppy dogs, are eager to learn and to please their masters. Both enjoy being with their owner and relish the affection and attention given to them. They like human company sufficiently to come up to you when you visit them in the paddock or in their box, so that teaching them anything should present little problem. But, and this has to be remembered, being young 'children', they lack lengthy concentration and frequently have no idea what is wanted of them, or even what you are trying to get at.

Colts and fillies that have followed the mare at foot until they have been weaned, and have then been kept together with others of a like age as yearlings and over and who have not been constantly handled each day, require considerable mental adjustment when they are suddenly confronted with individual attention and are first subjected to personal discipline. It is true that they will come up to a human as members of a group, but the hard work usually begins as soon as you wish to lay hands on them.

Animals rising four years and over which are suddenly expected to perform, even at the end of a lunge rein, or those which have been mishandled — by which I do not mean cruelly treated — or those which have been badly broken or have learned no manners at all, require great tact, patience and careful handling, as well as some insight into the causes of their personal problems if they are to be taught anything at all, or if they have to be re-made.

The same rules apply in the teaching of any of these animals. The basic requirements are tact, patience, an understanding that you are working with a horse not a human being, a teaching concept which has been carefully worked out and is followed consequentially, and a willingness to expend time in order to ensure that the lesson is firmly fixed in the pupil's mind. By this I mean that the pupil should not be rushed nor over-tired by too-long learning sessions, and that sometimes it may take a week or two before the lesson is really grasped. The trainer very soon gets to know when the pupil is resisting, or when it plainly does not understand what is wanted.

Many of the exercises in this book entail working the horse at a distance, and it is essential to remember that a horse, especially a young one, wants to be near to his trainer physically, even to touch him, so in distance work the pupil must first be taught that it is not being deserted.

I use a number of aids to help overcome this problem, from 'touching canes' to plain honest bribery. But the foundation to working successfully with a horse, or any animal for that matter, is personal trust and how you treat it when it is at home or not working. I am very much for bribery in helping to condition reflexes, but otherwise against tit-bits except when given at certain stated times. A bribe is simply a reward, but it is linked with an activity and is given when the horse reacts as desired. Tit-bits given freely tend to make the horse demanding, even to the point of becoming angry or fractious when it does not get one.

For those who have been told that horses are difficult to manage, or who have been scared into thinking they are nothing but walking problems, let me say that this is not so. There are rules to good horse management, but they are common sense. Properly educated horses present few, if any, problems and those that are sensibly cared for are not, as one is sometimes led to believe, always at the vet's. All my horses have been kept as pets, but with certain very clear reservations: the major one of which is that I am the boss animal, the refuge and the one who calls the tune. For my part of the deal I never raise my voice, never strike my horse, never force it against its natural fears but show it instead how to overcome them. And all of that is plain common sense. I know my horses better because I am their friend and tutor, and if I go into a box and sit in the straw for a quarter of an hour or so, I expect the horse to come and talk to me, and not to climb up the back wall in order to get away from me.

All this has to do with establishing personal relations through education as well as understanding more or less what goes on in the animal's head. This is what my book is all about.

References

1. WYNMALEN, HENRY, *Equitation*, J.A. Allen & Co. Ltd, London, 1971.

CHAPTER 8

The Tutor

ANYBODY WHO HOPES TO TEACH any animal anything has to first take a look at himself and his motives. For this reason I start with the tutor before ever mentioning the pupil. The tutor has to define his objectives long before he starts work, and he has to keep to them. Education is never an easy matter, and in the case of horses certain pressures may well determine the course that is taken. These pressures include the age of the animal, how soon it has to be ready for use, its personality and temperament and, above all, the ability of the tutor in relation to all of the factors that arise.

In writing this book I am assuming that the tutor is working for himself or a friend, and is concerned with either a very young horse or with the re-education of an older one that does not come up to the expectations of the owner. Most horses that show problems have either been badly or hurriedly broken and have learned all about defences against the will of their handlers. Horses have no hesitation when it comes to getting their own way, or in trying to do so.

Education takes time. There are no short cuts, and no hurried programme will achieve lasting results. Because there are no genius horses, but merely intelligent or stupid ones, the longer the initial time available in teaching them anything, the more lasting the results. So, even the simplest of lessons can only become effective if time is devoted to it, and this has to be backed up by an almost endless fund of patience, self-control and understanding of the particular problems with which the pupil is faced. Not all problems are alike to all horses, nor are all horses the same. Their reactions to the same things, or similar situations, may be totally different.

Everybody who decides to educate his own horse should bear in mind that one senseless crack of the whip, or cut from the polo whip, one fit of bad temper or shouting, or one outbreak of arrogant impatience, may well undo hours of patient work, or even worse, destroy the trust that has been carefully built up and is so essential in teaching. A horse will not understand such outbursts but will sense human upset quite clearly through the lead rein, or the reins in the rider's hands, as quickly as it will through its trainer's outward demonstrations.

If we make rules for our pupil or pupils, we must also make rules for ourselves concerning our behaviour, our methods and our personal approach. This is because we are dealing with a living being that is a sensitive creature with an often high degree of intelligence, a limited ability to think conceptually, plus an astonishing memory which is not only general, but which also includes detail. For this reason, we frequently must take time to 'explain' things to our pupil, especially if a young one.

As my interest and work with horses is mainly concerned with equine-human relationships, equine character and intelligence, the system and approach to the handling and education of young horses, as well as to the animals themselves, is naturally based upon it. Experience has taught me that the first thing a tutor must concern himself with is the personal character of his pupil. You must learn something about its nature during the first four days that the horse comes to you. It is even better if you can visit the animal in its stable before it ever comes to your yard, and see how it behaves towards its owners; but this, of course, is not always possible.

The prudent tutor will not make his teaching sessions long and wearisome, but will keep up the interest by varying the lessons during each session and day by day afterwards. Thus lesson A, started on Monday, is only repeated on Wednesday and possibly on Friday, while lesson B is reserved for Tuesday, Thursday and Saturday, and the whole rota changed for the following week, with very little time devoted to any lesson at the outset. There is so much to teach a green horse that the tutor will always find something that has to be done, and in that way make the routine of lessons random. A couple of minutes per lesson is all that is needed at first if the horse is not to be soured.

There is great virtue in getting the feel of when a lesson should be broken off, and wisdom in breaking off a lesson that is not going well but in such a manner as to prevent the pupil noticing the reason for it. Horses share the common fate of their tutor in having good and bad days, and the good teacher does not persist on what are obviously bad days, when the pupil appears to be totally incapable of concentration.

It is variety that makes the horse and keeps it alert and interested. Certainly not the same routine, day after day.

The tutor's golden rules are as follows, and he must never allow himself to slip up and forget them:

(1) The horse has a phenomenal memory.
(2) The horse is a highly sensitive animal.
(3) No matter how marvellously intelligent the pupil may appear to be, or to become, no matter how affectionate and obedient and understanding it may be, it remains, first and foremost, a horse. It thinks as a horse, acts as a horse, and behaves within all of the limitations of its nature. Then, when the unexpected happens and we believe all we have taught has been in vain, we have to remember that the horse's instincts, reflexes and mechanisms are a part

of the animal's heritage and cannot be *basically* changed by even the most careful education. They may, at best, only be controlled.

(4) Never humanise the horse. Humanising within this context means to demand feats of understanding that are beyond the horse's mental capacity, no matter how high it may be. A horse that is humanised, and this happens more often then one thinks, will have more problems than those that are spurned, rebuffed or regarded as 'only an animal'.

(5) Never lose one's temper with a horse; never shout at it, nor hit it senselessly.

(6) Never try to force a horse by strength or by brutality, for this is a sure way to spoil it. It will put up defences against ill treatment and because of its superior strength, of which it is not conscious, will win the argument. After this it knows what to do, and can only be countered by fear, something we do not wish to induce at any cost.

Finally, a word to anybody who is stepping into the shoes of the tutor for the first time. It is vital to remember that horses are not, as has been said often enough, stupid animals. Remember that there is an enormous communications gap between the human and the equine species. This can only be partially closed by building up a very close relationship based on mutual respect and trust. The tutor should bear in mind that it is he who is demanding from the horse and not the latter who is asking to be taught. On the contrary. The pupil would like nothing better than to spend its life in the paddock rather than learning things that go against the promptings of its nature and without which it could do very well. Nevertheless, a properly handled horse will wake up and show eager interest and an enormous willingness to learn. It will not be able to put it into words, but it will quickly demonstrate its pleasure in the company of its contact person and handler. Properly handled horses will learn almost anything within reason and be a pleasure to own.

CHAPTER 9

The Horse

THE PRIMARY OBJECT in educating the horse is to fit it out
for its place in human society. We do not have to bother
about its place within the equine group, as the horses look
after that themselves when they have established and
accepted their rank, even within a small domestic herd.
Badly educated horses, or those that have had no education
at all, are a potential danger to themselves and to those who
have to deal with them. They are social misfits in so far as
they have not been taught how to behave themselves when
out, or will not readily come under control should they be
frightened.

Domestic horses should be steady, reliable and good
friends. It is a great advantage to start with a young animal
that has not been backed, but older horses that are not quite
as one would like them to be, may be readily re-educated.
This is especially so in the case of horses that are kept alone,
for they will quickly become tractable and good companions
to their human partner. Because, generally speaking, they
are kind, generous, willing and mostly quick on the uptake,
it takes them little time to recognise their true friends, and

even a difficult horse will settle down well and learn if it is properly handled.

I have certain golden rules where horses are concerned. They are so simple and undemanding that even horses which come to stay in my yard for a few weeks are subjected to them. It is a question of teaching the rules and making the horse live by them. These rules may be taught and assimilated in a very short time.

(1) The horse must learn to walk obediently and in a straight line in-hand. It is surprising how many do not do this when it is demanded of them.

(2) The horse must come to you in its box and allow its headcollar to be put on or taken off with ease.

(3) The horse must move over in the box when asked to do so. This is very important at those times when the animal is confined to the box for any reason and the box has to be mucked out, or the animal fed.

(4) The horse must stand in the door of its box or in the stable passage when told to do so. This seems to be a difficult lesson to learn and even my mare Tirade has broken trust and wandered off when my back has been turned. But, generally speaking, there is not much of a problem in teaching the horse to stand still and to give its hooves, one by one, for picking and inspection, without having to be tied up.

(5) The horse must trust my voice and be made to understand that there is no need of fear when I, and later its rider, are with it. This is far less difficult to teach than one might be led to believe.

(6) The horse must come to the paddock or meadow entrance when called. To let them get away with not doing so and to try and catch them, is to allow them a certain dominance that I will not tolerate. This is one of my strictest rules. I would rather not use the horse than capitulate and go up to it.

(7) The horse must learn that I am the herd leader and threat postures cut no ice. I will get what I want very quietly, but with utmost insistence.

These are the basic golden rules for the horse, and to my mind the most important in its preliminary education. It is not necessary to make a meal of teaching them. A couple of well-spent minutes each day, and I literally mean a couple of minutes, are all that is required. But the teaching must be consistent and spread over a period so that the rules are driven permanently into the individual's head. Horse A may get the basics firmly into its head in only two weeks, whereas horse B may require up to two months to do so. But the lessons should be repeated even after the tutor is positive that they have struck home.

The basis of success in teaching is an established mutual trust between horse and tutor. Neither should fear the other at any time or in any situation. The animal will become relatively difficult, or even unmanageable, if it senses its teacher is afraid of it, or of anything. Dominance by the human partner is by conviction, by implanting the feeling that he will always be the person to go to in times of real or imagined danger, and by the feeling that if he, the tutor, can approach an object of fear without drawing back from it, everything is in order.

It has to be remembered at all times that horses are sensitive in the extreme, by which I mean that nervousness may be transferred to them by touch, through the reins or simply by vibration. I have dealt with this sort of ESP in Chapter 6.) I have proved to my own satisfaction by repeated experiments, that a horse may be calmed by putting out a hand, yet not touching it. Important, at all times, is the tone and pitch of the human voice, which, according to my observations, is insufficiently used by most people when dealing with animals. Reaction to a familiar voice is instantaneous, but the voice must be calm as well as low-pitched, even when reproving.

The equine pupil will become interested and try to learn as soon as you begin to teach it anything. If it does not learn quickly, then it is due to one of two reasons: either the teaching – the 'explanation' – is wrong; or the animal is not too gifted and requires time to learn by repetition. I have not yet met an unwilling pupil, unless it has been spoiled, and even then the tutor may convince the horse that he wishes it no harm, providing he keeps his patience and inspires it with confidence.

R.S. Summerhays lists thirty-one problems in twenty-six chapters within the pages of his book *The Problem Horse*.[1] In my opinion, most of these problems need not exist if the horse is educated with consideration and patience. The fact that this excellent book has gone through six editions suggests that the same mistakes are made repeatedly. Admittedly, many of them may be traced to indifferent or inexpert and illogical handling, resulting from lack of knowledge concerning the psyche of the species. It is my belief that more horses are spoiled through lack of understanding than by deliberate cruelty.

References

I.   SUMMERHAYS, R.S., *The Problem Horse*, J.A. Allen & Co. Ltd, London, 1975.

CHAPTER 10

Newcomers to the Stable

ONE SHOULD NOT BE LED TO BELIEVE that a change of stable, even if for the better, is a matter of indifference to the horse. However good the box provided or the conditions offered, many animals have considerable problems as far as adjustment is concerned. The fact remains that a change of personnel and dwelling may be a considerable shock to the individual's mental and nervous system.

As soon as the new horse is led down from the trailer to step cautiously into a new way of life, a whole series of factors are already awaiting its arrival. The most important of these is that it is coming into a totally unfamiliar world, peopled by strangers. It is not aware of this at first. It is not aware of potential permanence. But everything looks different, smells and sounds different, and the change is enormous, especially in the case of a young horse that has never experienced anything of this nature before.

Realisation of its new situation begins to dawn the second or third day of its arrival when it discovers that it has lost its old friends. They have vanished out of its life forever.

There is not a single human being that it loves or trusts, not a single familiar horse, and if it comes as a lone horse, to be kept as such, it will suffer loneliness and boredom. Everything it has known has been suddenly swept away; it is out on its own and it has to deal with the situation. It becomes a creature in need of support and help.

Because they become bewildered, even insecure, many horses will attempt to cover up their anxiety by sulking or by defending themselves by shows of aggression – fake threat postures – or by excessive shyness and timidity. Therefore, all horses that are new to a stable must be handled with extra consideration and tact during the vital first four days. Sympathy extended during that period will pay dividends.

When a horse, young or old, is introduced to its new home, the first thing it will usually do is to inspect its quarters minutely. It will sniff at the bed, the manger, the salt block, and at anything within range that may give it a clue as to the lie of the land. Some will look out of the stable window; some will look out over the half door. Others will stand stock still and deposit a pile of droppings, or urinate. The droppings should be picked up with a fork and deposited in a corner of the box and left there until the next day. I usually put a thin covering of straw over them in order to keep away flies. Those droppings will be added to by the many that follow during the next few hours and will mark the box as the animal's very own.

I have always made a practice of giving any newcomer a pound of oats the moment that it is introduced to its new home. This will usually settle the animal and occupy it until the transport and its people have left the yard. It is very important that the person who will be handling the animal is the one who *brings* the oats to it. The newcomer must not *find* this snack; it *must* be given to it. The person who gives this tit-bit should be the future tutor in the case of animals that are going to be educated. After the oats, a couple of pounds of well-pulled hay will help to occupy the newcomer for a time after it has been left alone.

It may take ten days for the animal fully to settle down and become acclimatised to its new surroundings, and about four to five days for it partially to accept its new people, by which time, unless the animal suffers from some overriding complex of which you are not aware, you ought to be getting along together well enough. I once had an old mare that simply refused to make friends for weeks and who regarded me as someone to be suffered because I was the source of food. Later, when she did accept me, she proved to be a wonderful friend and would do anything that I asked of her.

I normally leave a newcomer confined to its box for the first four days. I would certainly not risk putting it out in a paddock; instead I take it out for exercise in-hand, about which I will say more later on.

Confinement to the box and in-hand exercise helps the horse get to know you, by recognising your voice, accepting your personal scent, learning to identify and look forward to your visits by the sound of your footsteps, becoming accustomed to your hands and your general method of approach, all of which will be different from that to which it has been accustomed.

Without depriving any other horse or horses that you may own of your usual attentiveness, those first days should be largely concentrated upon the newcomer. Visit him in his box, and if he shows signs of accepting you, squat down in the straw and allow him to examine you as minutely as he pleases. He will do this if you do not rebuff him, and allowing him to do so will build up his confidence.

The second day after his arrival should be devoted to an orientation walk. I show the horse the yard. Many stables are so arranged that the animal has little chance to look out of a window and to find out what the outside world is like. So I show new youngsters their surroundings in order that they may become familiar with them and learn where their stable is. Also there will be many things about the new home that are totally strange and quite outside the animal's experience and he may feel bewildered or frightened by them. So the first orientation walk may be quite a hectic affair, with the young horse, or even an old one, snorting and shying at the most everyday things.

As soon as I notice anything that is exciting interest or fear, I approach it slowly, touch it with my free hand, and then allow the horse to inspect it at his leisure, which he will do after several fearful and tentative attempts. I will make soothing sounds and tell him it is 'all right', coaxing him to smell and feel whatever the object is, be it a water butt or tractor.

These leisurely tours of the yard and, if all goes quietly, the immediate vicinity, will be the horse's first lesson in trusting me, my lack of fear of anything establishing me in the pupil's mind as very much the Alpha animal. And I will make a point of investigating and demonstrating everything and anything that comes along for the next two years, or more. In doing so, it will never be necessary to force the animal against its deeper instincts, and I will save the rider a great deal of trouble when the pupil finally comes under saddle. There is no doubt about it – a certain phlegm may be taught most horses, making them good to ride and more certain as competition animals.

Each succeeding day will increase the scope of our strolls of inspection, and I find that my charge will go readily back to its stable after sniffing at motor cars, feeling the texture of the refuse bins, having a look at one or other of the loose-boxes and even having been inside them to get to know the scent of the other horse or horses, and spending a few minutes at the hitching rail where all horses are groomed or quartered. Nor have we neglected to make our way as far as the paddocks in order to get to know how to get there and back.

After the fourth day, the newcomer, now more certain of its tutor and the surroundings, is put out in a paddock on its own. He will feel the grass under his feet and exercise himself, while I stand by the rail and call encouragement to him. He will gallop about, stand and look, trot, graze a little, walk a while, have another little trot and then wander around on his own tour of inspection, familiarising himself with the lie of the land until he discovers the horse, or horses, in the neighbouring paddock. He may even call a greeting, but not necessarily so. I leave him to his own devices once he has settled and will not return to him until I wish to put him back in his box after an hour or two.

He will usually come willingly when called, because he wants the nearness of his contact person.

I follow this routine for a few days until I judge the time ripe to bring him right up to his neighbours on the leading rein, so that he may touch noses with them at the paddock rail. He is bound to become a little excited because of the contact, and there may be squealings and pawings with the forefeet, but when we have done this once or twice, I introduce him into the paddock with the other horses and let them get on with the business of becoming fully acquainted and of establishing their own rank.

There will probably be some shows of aggression, with the laying back of ears and biting and, if you have only mares, lightning quick lashings out of the hindquarters and even kicks. There will be great unrest for some days with frequent threat displays whenever contact is made or one or other parties gets too close, for they will mostly be careful to graze at some distance from each other. However, if there are only two horses they will regulate the social precedence soon enough. Although they may not accept one another for quite a long time, they are really incapable of staying away from each other too long and will seem to keep an uneasy truce interspersed with putting back the ears and making threatening faces. But even during that stage, whichever animal is put out first will be standing waiting for the arrival of the other.

I make a point of inspecting the animals in the paddock as time allows during the day, and the horses will either come to me of their own accord, or I will go into the paddock to talk to them. There may be some shows of jealousy because each of the paddock's occupants has long ago decided that I am its personal property and friend. They may both attempt to crowd me a bit, which must not be allowed, and they soon come to recognise the fact that neither will go short of the desired affection.

I make a great rule of forbidding the giving of any tit-bits in the paddock, because of the danger of making the horses snappy and greedy. Only my wife breaks this rule, and both our animals appear to accept this because they never look for anything from me or from anyone else who deals with them.

Because I am interested in educating young horses or those that have been spoiled and require re-education and schooling and because I am not working commercially, I find myself in the happy position of having time on my side. I am preoccupied with increasing the animal's store of knowledge in such a manner that it will not forget anything it has been taught. I may work slowly, even spasmodically if I so choose, secure in the knowledge that the pupil's phenomenal memory is working with me, even if the pupil is unaware of this.

In general, I can reckon on a year or two of patient work, so that by the time that I am finished, the green horse will be a very agreeable character to back and make under saddle.

Older horses that I have had in my care usually belonged to friends, were retired, or in need of rest as a result of injury, and they were all made to conform to my rules. While I have never had a 'guest' horse that has measured up to any that I have taught, most of my visitors learned very quickly, even when they were no longer young, and I never had trouble with any of them.

I do not begin to work with a new young horse until it has been with me for a month or so. I want it to lead a very pleasant life, and although I will be teaching it almost all of the time, even when leading it out to the paddock, I will not go in for obvious lessons, but will merely condition it to follow and respect me.

During the early days, the main thing is to make the horse know it is at home.

CHAPTER 11

Leading

IT IS ESSENTIAL for good management, that horses allow themselves to be properly led. In spite of this, you do come up against animals that are difficult on the lead rein. Some become excited at the prospect of being put out in the paddock or in strange surroundings, some are listless and move in a slovenly way, and not a few defend themselves against the leading hand.

Horses that resist the leading hand and behave badly are exceedingly trying and even dangerous. This is especially so if they have been confined indoors for any length of time. Therefore, the earlier they learn to allow themselves to be led properly, the better it is for all concerned. Every horse should go in a straight line and in a relaxed manner when being led. This is fundamental to all work in hand. We shall see how important it is when we come to discuss some of the disciplines like lungeing and work on long reins, or even walking as a means of developing mind and muscle.

Many people like their horses to be a bit showy when being led. They feel that an animal that is nervy and agitated at the end of the lead rein is exhibiting some of the fire that is within. Some show judges are impressed by this kind of behaviour, so that one is advised to increase the oats before presenting the animal in-hand. Nineteenth-century horse dealers were wont to achieve this form of mettlesomeness by inserting a piece of ginger into the unfortunate animal's rectum, so causing a discomfort that made even the laziest nonentity pick up its feet, prick its ears and dance about.

My personal preference is for a horse that leads well because it is quiet and handy on account of its good manners, but is alive and active when performance is demanded of it. I like a horse to be so that I can stop for a chat, if I am leading it, without it fidgeting around like a badly brought up child. Spirit and high courage are shown when the horse is being worked, not necessarily at the wrong moment in the wrong place.

It is unpleasant to have an animal that tries to be boss, or that jogs along, or that breaks away from the handler or that simply resists by the use of certain tricks. The horse must not be allowed to succeed in gaining the upper hand. If it does, the animal could become unmanageable, especially if it ever becomes really scared.

Lucky are those who begin with a foal and decide how it is to be educated. They will have an animal that goes on the lead rein like an old hand by the time it is six months old.

The late Henry Wynmalen suggested a teaching method in his book on horse breeding and stud management[1], that I have used with great success. When the foal is a couple of days old, the handler enters the box with an assistant who secures the mare with a headcollar. The handler places one arm around the foal's chest and the other around the quarters, and allows the animal to fight him. It will do this by struggling. Care has to be taken to remain firm but passive during this procedure, for the little animal must not be frightened. The foal, being weaker than the person holding it, will give up the struggle after a minute or so. The mare is then led around the box by the assistant, and a soft stable rubber passed around the neck of her foal, which is then led after her, the handler helping it forward and controlling it with the arm around the quarters.

Thereafter the foal is never allowed to follow the mare on its own, whether being taken out to the paddock or being brought back to its box. The stable rubber is always placed around the neck and the controlling hand around the quarters, and the pupil is urged to walk beside or behind the mare. Within a few days, the handler may put his right hand over the foal's back at a point near the quarters, and later on, use the right hand against the shoulder of the charge. The mare must be led quietly and sensibly by somebody who does not rush her and who is able to keep an eye on the foal and whoever is leading it.

I put the first headcollar on the foal when it is three or four weeks old and already familiar with this leading routine, but I do not make use of a rein. I slip the fingers of my left hand between cheek and cheek strap instead. The first lead rein is not used until the foal is pretty steady when being led the short distance of a hundred or so metres from stable to paddock. The mare is always led well into the paddock and made to stand until the foal is released; and it is my practice to make the foal stand for a few seconds when I say 'Stand', before letting it go. This will prove its worth later on when the foal is older and you want it to stand and stay, whatever the reason. The result is a very handy little creature that will come up to you with squeals of pleasure whenever you put in an appearance by the paddock rail. To my mind, you can do nothing but good for the animal if you handle it in this way.

When the foal has passed the inevitable stage of darting forward, standing still, skittering about and trying to get to its mother, you may attach a lead rein and, with your right hand over its back, have it walk along beside you. As soon as it has learned that it will be free to join its dam in the paddock and goes along willingly, you can lead it properly on the rein, always keeping that consoling and controlling right hand on or near the shoulder.

There should be no problem with horses that have been

educated in this way, if the handler is quiet and patient and amused by the task of teaching them. I still look back with pleasure on the day when I saw a young African student at the Irish National Stud, trying to lead an exceedingly lively little thoroughbred foal by its headcollar. He flashed a delightful and delighted smile in my direction, and the fun that he was having with the troublesome youngster was such that he felt compelled to share it with somebody else. But the situation is somewhat different with a horse which has not been taught this way and which may not even have been taught at all.

Bad behaviour while being led is really unnecessary. To my mind, leading is the number one discipline and it has to be right. No matter how high-couraged or full of fire the individual may be, it has to be quiet and obedient on the lead rein. Its hot blood is no excuse. It must be quiet up to the moment that it is brought into the paddock, turned to the rail and let loose. Only then may it thunder off to buck and kick up its heels joyously.

It will happen that even the most obedient and disciplined horse will skitter when being led, but the cause may usually be identified and the temporary excitement laid by the handler's voice.

Many of the faults that are encountered, spring from incorrect handling or inexpert teaching. Coming in on, or breaking out from, the leading hand require correction; such faults may be more readily attributed to the handler than to the animal and, as will be seen with many of the faults that I am about to deal with, stem from a basic error on the part of the handler.

It is a psychological fact that horses do not like to be led short, just as it is a fact that they would prefer not to be led at all. Unfortunately, you cannot always rely upon a horse to walk free by your side, or to heel, although mine are sometimes encouraged to do so. The temptation to follow the true dictates of their nature is mostly too great and they will wander off to take a look at things or to nibble at a tuft of grass.

A horse that is led short puts up an automatic defence against the leading hand. This is most probably due to the fact that a short-held rein restricts the natural balance and pendulum action of the head and neck, so essential to comfortable movement. Remember that a horse is constantly changing its centre of gravity as it moves, while balancing itself with its head and neck.

Coming in on the hand, or breaking out and away from it, are basically the same thing. It starts at the head and neck, with the latter arching to bring the head nearer to the leading hand, but also bending it towards it. This leads to the whole body angling away from the hand, i.e., the handler, leaving the animal no alternative but to walk or trot side-ways. If you persist in leading short, you will create other leading troubles, like jogging and overbending. The remedy is so simple: lengthen the rein, drop back a pace to the level of the shoulder, and the animal will usually walk in a straight line.

I contend that most leading faults are due to this simple root, believing that the majority of problems may be over-come by simply giving the horse more rein, because, believe it or not, you have more *control* through a longer rein.

One of the faults that may be born of too-short leading, is that of circling. Most young horses that have not been led as foals or handled sufficiently, will use this as a defence. They will come in on the leading hand, cross in front of the handler and circle him. The remedy is to lengthen the rein and allow the horse to come in, but then to force it to circle you close, as often as you decide, which is not what the animal wanted to do in the first place. This 'bending' the horse around you causes it difficulty, and why this is so will be discussed later in the chapter on lungeing. The next step is to lead the horse out of the unwanted circles, in the direction that you were going. Attempts at circling will probably be made from time to time and will be corrected in the same manner on each occasion, but, being clever, most horses get the message pretty soon and give up the idea. I usually carry the game a little bit further by standing still at some point and forcing the pupil to circle me when it doesn't want to do anything of the sort. You may make a little capital out of breaking the habit of wilfully circling, because, in a sense, you introduce the first principles of lungeing while doing so, but lungeing lessons are not the object of everyday leading.

Another defence against the leading hand is the unpleasant manoeuvre of swinging around to face the handler, lifting the head and pulling away backwards in a kind of tug-o'-war. Spectators love this sort of thing. I will not tolerate it. It is often seen in groups of led stallions, when one of their number becomes excited and infects the next and the whole string begins to kick up heels and fight against the handlers. A lone animal may be dealt with easily enough, providing that the lead rein is long enough.

If an animal does this to me, I let it have plenty of rein, then gather it in and, while doing so, come alongside the shoulder and lead it forward in a straight line, right back in the direction from whence we have come. I then turn as soon as the horse is walking properly and go back in the direction that I want to go. I consider it no waste of time to repeat this whenever the horse tries to make a fresh attempt, playing at this game as long as the horse does so and talking to it calmly during the proceedings. Excitement is usually the cause of this behaviour. I do nothing else to make it accept my own terms. Persistence wins in the end. No tug-o'-war. I do *nothing* beyond what I have already described, except to use my voice very gently and conversationally, to distract the animal's attention. Some horses need a sharply spoken 'Lah' or 'No', or whatever sound one makes when expressing displeasure, and that makes them come to hand.

There is also the defence that is best described as throwing up the head and digging in the heels. I part-owned a very big and excellent mare, who was shy of her head. She was very, very obstinate and excitable, and would wilfully shy her head and dig in her heels when she wanted her way. She made things a bit more difficult by dropping her quarters and straightening her front legs. I had seen her being beaten for doing this before I bought her. The whip is useless in such situations. It will either frighten badly and make the animal almost unmanageable, or help to make it even more difficult to lead normally.

The first time she did this to me, I had no idea what I should do, so I pulled against her on the rein. She leaned one way and I the other, and I came up against the full weight of her resistance. The harder I pulled, the harder she did. Then I stumbled on the answer by accident. Disgusted, I suddenly let go of the rein when our struggle was at its peak. She almost fell over backwards. Her head came down as she fought for balance, and I was there with the rein in my hand when she found it. She followed me like a lamb. But she had not yet learned her lesson. She put up this unpleasant defence repeatedly, either when being led indoors, or when she wanted to remain out in the paddock. The whole business was very irritating when I wanted to get her in quickly out of pouring rain, or in a thunderstorm, when I will never leave a horse out of doors. I had to work out a reasonable method.

Because I neither beat nor shout at horses it remained open to me to use my brain. No horse, I reasoned, is capable of keeping its head up indefinitely. It would therefore be a reasonable assumption that the best way to make the head come down would be to do the easiest thing of all, which is nothing. Or, alternatively, if one had to do something, force the head to *remain* up there by exerting gentle control with the rein, while tickling, but only tickling, the animal under the jawbone with the little lash at the end of the dressage whip. I tried both systems, and found that letting the horse get its head down on its own was quicker and more effective. As soon as the head does come down, the horse is made to do a *volte*, out of which it is quietly led forward. The end result is that nobody's nerves are frayed and, by repetition, the horse can be made to see that the whole business is nonsense. The 'I can wait longer, I have all the time in the world' attitude of the handler wins every time, and such a horse eventually loses altogether the inclination to resist.

Horses will sometimes suddenly stand stock still and refuse to go forward. I wait a moment the first time this happens and watch the head. If the head is given a little shake and there is no alertness about the eyes and ears, it usually means that the animal is determined to have its own way. If it will not budge after reasonable vocal encouragement, I give it a hard slap on the shoulder with the back of my hand. If it makes a habit of this sort of thing, I carry a dressage whip in my left hand, point back, and give a sharp little tap behind where the girth of the saddle would normally be. Care has to be taken that the horse does not *see* where the little sting is coming from. If the horse is alert, ears forward, head slightly raised, eyes looking into the middle distance, I look myself in order to find possible causes of anxiety. Should the apparent reason be close enough, I will walk ahead of my charge, paying out rein, then touch and *talk* to whatever it is. The horse will usually follow very cautiously, its nostrils distended and sometimes even snorting, especially if it is an Arab, to satisfy itself that there is no real danger. The idea must always be to get the charge to have a close look and smell for itself.

If the object is not within reach, it is wise to wait until the horse satisfies itself that the source of its temporary fear is harmless. If whatever it is moves away then the horse will calm down. If the object that excites the fear is stationary and merely unfamiliar, the animal will remain suspicious, but also calm down. Of course, the handler should reassure all the time and 'infect' the horse with his own calm. He can then lead the horse up to the object and allow an inspection. The main thing is never to force.

Another problem is the animal that pulls like a steam engine. Although this is normally due to excitement, or wanting to get somewhere in a hurry, or some such cause, it is basically due to bad early education. Pulling may become a habit if the handler has trouble dealing with it. The horse can be led on a snaffle bridle if the habit is really bad, but there is a problem here when you get to the paddock and want to slip the horse loose. It is best to lead such horses out behind a calm and experienced schoolmaster, provided one is available. Pulling is difficult to break and it may be necessary to give the animal a leading course on the bridle and reins. The offside rein should be about a centimetre shorter than the inside one, but both reins should be held relatively long and the leading hand should be where the throat and chest unite. Many forward-moving horses exhibit this habit, which may also be a combination of ambition to go and real excitement. I once had a very strong four-year-old Westphalian of some seventeen hands, who was very difficult to manage. Although it took a little while, I did eventually get him handy on the lead rein by leading him behind a schoolmaster.

Joggers and dancers appeal to some people because they look showy and, if one doesn't know better, full of life and fire. This up-on-the-toes and skittering comes, in my opinion, from too-short leading of well-bred and nervous animals. They are always looking about them to see what is going on and may well step on the handler's toes, if he doesn't take care. I talk to such horses all the time, trying to distract their attention from everything except myself, but this will only partially stop them dancing about. The fault must be dealt with in the school and the horse taught to walk properly.

Re-schooling on the lunge will go a long way towards getting things right, if the trainer is calm and persistent. Walking will also help to lay this kind of excitability. I would personally start from scratch, first by ordinary leading, then parallel leading (see Chapter 15) for a while, followed by ordinary lungeing with careful moments of trot and canter inserted between longer sessions of ordinary walk. Such work must be calm and controlled and demanding rhythm rather than speed, at all paces. The calming effect of the voice is immensely important.

Once the horse shows that it will go calmly – in other words, that it has gained a certain confidence – it should go under a rider, who would be well advised to follow the suggestions of R. S. Summerhays[2] who recommends sitting loosely in the saddle in order to relax the animal and gently reining every time it attempts to break from walk to trot or jog. The reins are loosened when the horse responds.

There are some sloppy individuals that have to be pulled along. This is the handler's fault and easily remedied by walking at the shoulder, holding the rein in the left hand and slapping the shoulder with the back of the right hand, or by holding the rein in the right hand and tapping with the end of the dressage whip. It seems to be more of a habit with obstinate ponies, than with horses. Although ugly, it is not dangerous, unless the animal takes it into its head to run you down. It should not take more than a week or two to correct this fault. Pieces of carrot and judicious tapping with the dressage whip are good aids.

In this, as in other individual faults, the handler's gentle voice will go a long way in correcting it. It is curious how shy many people are when it comes to talking to their animals. The human voice is a valuable aid in reassuring and in distracting attention away from all sorts of outside influences.

Horses that resort to defence should never be punished, and a whip should not be used under any circumstances whatever, except as a gentle aid. Nor should the handler's voice ever be raised above a normal, quietly spoken reprimand. Although resistance may be tried repeatedly, the animal will eventually be dominated by its handler's patience and determination, through voice contact and that of the rein. Force cannot be met by force, for the horse will always win such an unequal struggle.

A final word about leading reins. I work with two lengths, 26 feet for unruly or impetuous animals, and 13 feet for everyday work. All reins are fitted with so-called 'panic', or quick-release, catches. This also applies to the lungeing rein. I have my short leading reins made specially by my saddler, from tough cotton and synthetic fibre webbing. There is a treble-thickness section sewn in between the release catch and a strong swivel, 4-6 inches below it. These leading reins can be washed and will be dry by the next day.

The rein used for leading should always be a long one in order to allow the animal to move away from the handler, or the handler away from the horse. Even the most peaceable animal may become a danger if it panics, and an injured handler is no use at all. Habitual pullers, horses which have had to be kept in their box for an overly long time due to injury, and animals which are new to the stable, should be led on the lunge rein in conjunction with a breaking cavesson. They are liable to become excited and impulsive when they first feel the ground under their feet, and there is no handling them unless you are properly equipped to do so. It is not enough to believe that you can, under such circumstances, handle even a trusted and beloved animal with impunity. In warning against the use of too-short leading reins under such conditions, or at any time for that matter, Diana Tuke[3] also underlines the dangers of injury to the handler.

I find that the way in which the leading rein is held can be of considerable help. The carefully looped rein should be held in the left hand (if one is leading from the left side) so that it can be run out in cases of emergency. The leading hand should be flat on top of the rein, with the thumb away from the shoulder of the led animal. This allows for greater control of the rein which, when necessary, may be pressed downwards, firmly but gently, not just to check but also to preserve mastery. In the case of an emergency, the rein should be allowed to run out from the left hand through the right with constant downward checks being used, as though one were applying a brake. Great care must be taken to prevent any section of the rein becoming looped around any limb of the handler. It is better to let go of the whole thing than come to injury in this way. But even the most excited and the heftiest horse may be controlled by the lunge rein and collected in afterwards.

Under normal circumstances, about 3 feet of rein should

separate the head of the horse from the leading hand. The handler should walk at the horse's shoulder with his forearm against the animal's side and his body slightly inclined towards his charge. He should walk in step with the horse. This will keep the rhythm fluid and will have the added advantage of preventing the horse treading on his feet.

References

1. WYNMALEN, HENRY, *Horsebreeding and Stud Management*, J. A. Allen & Co. Ltd, London, 1971.
2. SUMMERHAYS, R. S., *The Problem Horse*, J. A. Allen & Co. Ltd, London, 1975.
3. TUKE, DIANA, *Horse by Horse*, J. A. Allen & Co. Ltd, London, 1973.

CHAPTER 12

Training to Stand

No less an authority than R. S. Summerhays[1] asserts that not 'one in thousands' of English horses will stand still when dismounted and left on their own by their riders.

Having the horse stand is a question of elementary education, starting when the animal is a foal, as suggested in the chapter on leading. Getting the horse to stand is no art. Application on the part of the tutor is enough. As far as I am concerned, standing is an essential part of making any horse socially safe. A horse that stands, even if only for a few minutes, is a reasonable and obedient animal.

As in everything connected with education, not with training, I allow about a minute per session, or at the very most, three minutes. But fifteen to twenty seconds per day should be sufficient to teach the horse to stand within the framework of the door of its box, although the time devoted to the work will be increased as the days and weeks pass. I make a habit of repeating lessons from time to time, even when I consider that the animal has learned well, and it is probably these refresher lessons undertaken on the spur of the moment, anywhere, anytime and when the horse is of any age, that help to keep the discipline evergreen.

I do not know what methods other people use to achieve this, but I shall never forget the outstanding stallion Roma-dour II, who stood for half an hour, half in, half out of his open box at the Westphalian National Stud, Warendorf, while I modelled his head and neck. It has to be pointed out that a very wide stable passage was in front of him and that fully occupied boxes of other stallions were to the right, the left and in front of him. He had simply been told to stand, and stand he did, his only movement during the whole session being to reach over and sniff at the model of himself on the modelling stand. This impressed me as much as the splendid colt at Mr Pitt-Rivers' Tollard Arabian Stud, who stood without moving, framed by the open door of his box, while mares and geldings were led past him.

I make use of an open box door when teaching horses to stand, and wear a pair of soft-soled shoes. The animal is placed in the open door and told to stand. If it tries to advance, and it will inevitably try to do so, I press the sole of the shoe against the leg and repeat the word 'Stand'. This is done each time the pupil tries to advance. If it stands stock still for some seconds, a reward is immediately forthcoming.

That is the first simple stage, designed to make the pupil familiar with the meaning of the word by associating it with restraint. This lesson is given every two or three days at irregular times. If you do not use irregular times, the animal comes to associate standing with a particular time only, and horses have quite a strong feeling for time.

How quickly the pupil learns depends not only upon the tutor and his patience, but also upon the individual. It must learn the true meaning of the word, because the tutor is not only teaching a positive action, but linking it to a human word. When the pupil has learned the first stage, which is to stand at the open door of the box on demand, but *without* reward, and to obey the voice should it decide to move off, then the time is ripe to go to the next stage, which takes place in the yard.

Once in the open, we must remember that it is the herd

instinct that governs so much of the horse's behaviour. What the average pupil is most afraid of, is being left alone. It wants to be near to the lead animal – in this case, the tutor. What the tutor has to teach the pupil, is that he will never leave it alone if he is not putting it out in the paddock, and that if he should go away, it will only be for a very short time. This is exactly what one has to do when training gun-dogs to sit and stay, or to go down and wait. They, too, have to be convinced that they are not going to be deserted by their owners.

Once in the yard, the horse is made to face its own box, the door of which is open. The box is the animal's home and should it feel uneasy, it has the certainty that it will be able to seek refuge there. Given this sense of security, the horse will be more likely to concentrate on what the tutor wishes it to do. The horse should now be facing its box and the tutor facing the horse, which is made to stand some metres from the box entrance. The tutor should hold the cheek straps of the headcollar and say 'Stand'. The pupil will normally try to take a step forwards or backwards, but will not succeed, and may try to break out to the right or left. This is not very important during the first outside lesson, but the repetition of the word 'Stand' is. When the animal stands still and straight – see if you can hold it in place while you count to fifteen – reward it and put it back into its box. This lesson is repeated every now and again, never every day, until the horse stands still and in a straight line and does not fidget. When this happens, the training can be taken a step further, but it is tremendously important for the tutor to be utterly convinced that the horse is ready for the next stage. What the horse is learning must last him all his life; it must really stick.

I have read about methods that advocate anchoring the horse to a stone, or throwing the reins over the head so that they hang down to the ground in front of the animal, but I cannot agree with them because I do not feel that the pupil is really learning to stand on command, or that it is being taught full confidence in its teacher. I do not like things hanging down in front of horses, because, should they take flight, they may trip and come down or do some injury to themselves.

The next stage involves the use of the lead rein, held about 20 inches below the jaw as soon as the horse has been placed in the normal position used when holding the cheek straps. The horse should be told to stand. It is very probable that it will do so, but it could also happen that it feels at relative liberty and will attempt to move forward towards the handler. It should be told to go back and pressed backwards by the vee formed by the first two fingers of the left hand being pushed into its chest. It should then be told to stand.

It is not necessary to describe, stage by stage, how the lead rein is gradually lengthened as the horse improves and really learns what it is all about. Nor should it be necessary to stress the need to use the voice, to encourage and praise, or the need to finish each session with a suitable reward of bread or carrot. But one day the horse will stand quietly away from you at the full length of the rein, say four metres, and will do so every time that this is asked of it.

You have achieved this in the same way that a good trainer teaches the gun-dog; that is, by gradually increasing the distance between you and the pupil as you retreat backwards from it, repeating 'Stand', or 'Stand and stay', as you go. Should the animal's nerve give and it moves towards you, then replace it on the original spot and start the whole procedure again. It is a game of patience; nothing more or less. As soon as the pupil has grasped the lesson, further progress can be made, but still in the stable yard, which is now a familiar stamping ground and holds no terrors.

The lead rein and headcollar are replaced by a bridle, the horse is fitted with a surcingle and the first really free effort is made. The pupil has the reins taken over his head and fastened to the surcingle by a piece of string, designed to do no more than hold them in place. He is made to stand in the usual position while the trainer backs away from him, but remains in sight and encourages him with his voice.

Unless this is attempted too soon, it is ten to one that the pupil will remain in position. Naturally, the usual praise and reward should follow. When this has been practised over a number of widely spread days, the horse can be 'placed' on the yard in various unfamiliar directions and in different parts of the yard while the tutor goes off for a minute or two, say, into the stable to inspect something, then goes back to the pupil, caresses him and leaves again. When the pupil shows signs of becoming bored and restless, he is told to stand, and that is actually the moment to break off the lesson in order not to bully and sour him.

Some days after the last of these 'yard lessons', the horse should be taken out to the school or paddock, placed in the middle of what must appear to it to be nowhere, and told to stand. The tutor should then go to the paddock rail, his back to the pupil, calling 'Stand' over his shoulder as he goes, and talking to the animal in a quiet and steady voice. What I normally do is sit down, light a cigarette and half smoke it, which takes about seven and a half minutes. That is about as much time as you may reasonably demand of a horse to stand stock still and alone in the centre of a paddock. It then deserves great praise.

While we have been dealing with horses learning to stand alone when placed, nothing has been said about the other occasions when it is necessary for the animals to be made to stand. Such moments are during the daily grooming, whilst being attended by the vet or farrier, whilst alone at the hitching rail, whilst being saddled and bridled and whilst the rider is mounting.

Most of this teaching is done by open bribery: simply leaving the pupil for a few moments and giving it something when you return. This should be done unobtrusively and quietly. But whatever one does, the training principle is always the same: the slow, slow build-up until horse and moment are ripe. The tutor must teach the horse confidence and show confidence in the animal. One has to show confidence in order to get it. And one has to show trust.

Although I do not normally want an assistant, I am more

than happy to have one when the pupil has to learn to stand still while somebody gets up on its back. This can be a very alarming experience for a young horse and the surprise is best diminished if the tutor stands by its head during the procedure. A light young person is the best helpmate. He, or she, should put a foot in the stirrup, mount and lie across the saddle without ever attempting to sit in it. The horse is liable to start forward, but will come up against both hitching rail and tutor, whose business it is to quieten it and to give it a reward, while telling it to stand. I have usually prepared the pupil, long before it is backed, by laying an arm across its back, or by standing beside it and leaning my weight over the back; so the feeling is not quite unfamiliar and will not frighten the pupil. Mary Rose[2] points out that it is a good idea to have somebody stand on a mounting block *before* any attempt is made actually to sit on the horse's back, in order to accustom it to the idea of seeing somebody above the normal level. This is common sense when we consider that it is the unknown which is the main cause of horses being frightened.

Wynmalen[3] advocates putting the foot in the stirrup when the horse is standing still, rewarding and then repeating several times. This work is done inside the horse's box. The same procedure is followed in the open.

While following both Wynmalen's and Miss Rose's methods, for there are none to better them, I prefer to stand at the horse's head when it is first backed and to steady it in the same way as it was steadied when being taught to stand – by a hand on either side of the head at the cheek straps, with this difference: that it will be given something pleasant to eat while the work is being done.

The lessons should extend over several days, stage by stage. There should be no hurry in teaching the animal something that it will have to experience all its life. There should be no impetuosity on the part of the people teaching it, no wild swinging up and landing with a bump in the saddle; everything should be done slowly and carefully, and repeated, or broken off if the horse will not stand.

One of the most important moments is the acceptance by the pupil of the rider's weight on the stirrup. The action affects the horse's sides, back and belly, causing discomfort, even if only momentarily, which is what makes the horse move at the very moment that it should not do so.

During the early days of riding, the tutor should always hold the animal steady, until the rider has mounted and the pupil has learned that there is nothing to fear.

References

1.   SUMMERHAYS, R. S. *The Problem Horse*, J. A. Allen & Co. Ltd, London, 1975.
2.   ROSE, MARY, *Training Your Own Horse*, George Harrap & Co. Ltd, London, 1977.
3.   WYNMALEN, HENRY, *Equitation*, J. A. Allen & Co. Ltd, London, 1971.

CHAPTER 13

Making a Horse Whip-wise

I HAVE SEARCHED the literature that is available to me for some mention of how to make a horse what I describe as whip-wise. Both Wynmalen and Mary Rose specify the correct use of the whip, but I have found no advice on specifically training horses to accept the whip.

Alas, very many horses are whip-shy. Some are so badly afraid of the whip that they almost go berserk at the mere sight of one. I once part-owned a very fine mare which was the classic example of the ruined horse. She had been so mishandled in every respect that it was a wonder she could be approached at all. I was to enjoy myself getting her spiritually right and secure again and she taught me a great deal of what I know about handling horses. She was so scared of the whip that I had to hide it behind my back if I wished to pass it up to whoever was riding her, and I could not use a whip when lungeing her.

Somebody once told me that all horses are *instinctively* shy of the whip, and even Wynmalen tells us that horses instinctively regard it as an object of suspicion. The many experiments I have conducted over the past twelve years force me to disagree. I consider fear of the whip not to be instinctive but, generally, the result of a conditioned reflex of the first order. I still accept the theory of instinctive fear only insofar as it is natural to horses to be suspicious of *anything* that is in any way unfamiliar to them. No foal, no green youngster that I have handled or educated has ended up whip-shy.

Fear of the whip is not endemic. I would be in very deep trouble were this so. There is practically no phase in the education of a horse during which I do not make use of either a long dressage whip, or a 'touching cane'. Obviously, the cause of shyness, and then fear, is the manner in which the whip is first introduced to the animal and then handled, rather than its mere presence. If you make sudden movements with the whip or brandish it, if you are negligent in your approach to the horse, cracking or swishing the whip, then you stand a pretty good chance of making the horse shy of it. The same result could be achieved with a paper bag, a handkerchief or a rein that was waved about thoughtlessly. Fast, sudden movements of the hand, which cannot be assessed, will make any horse or animal nervous. It must be clear therefore that all hand movements, either with or without a whip, should always be on the slow and deliberate side, with care taken to make the intention clear.

It has always seemed important to me that the animal understands the nature of an object before it is asked to react to it. I like to use the horse's memory, powers of observation, uncanny sense of smell, good nature and willingness to learn as the main aids in teaching. I therefore use them when teaching about whips, which I classify as active and passive. The active whip is only used, and at that sparingly, when the horse is being ridden, so I only mention it in passing. The passive whip is something else and, as the name implies, does little except act as an extension of the hand, becoming what may be described as a long and gentle finger that directs and holds physical contact.

I know that a horse is not afraid when I pick up a pitchfork and go into the stable with it, any more than it is when I carry in a bucket, a stable rubber or a broom. There is therefore no good reason why the same horse should be afraid of a whip, even instinctively, when it is carried by the same familiar hand. Unless, of course, the horse had a previous bad experience with a whip or stick before it ever came into my hands.

If it is your intention to make a horse really whipwise, the first thing to do in setting about the work, is to carry a long dressage whip with you almost all of the time during the period of teaching. This will accustom the horse to the sight of the thing. It becomes a 'normal' part of you. Remember that the moment you come into the yard the horse will be observing you and your every movement with the keenest of interest. So, you can flick the whip about, or tuck it under your arm and march about with it, without causing any excitement or relating it to the horses.

Naturally enough, I make a point of going up to the half-door with the whip in my hand. I will not allow the occupant of the box to investigate it, or even touch it, but will lean it out of reach against the outside wall of the stable before going into the box. If I am taking the animal out, I will leave the whip there.

People say that horses are curious, but I say they like to be informed, and this withholding of the whip teases them. Some will make great attempts to reach the whip by stretching out as far as they can over the door: others will try to pull you over to it as you lead them out.

I will play this game for a few days with a green youngster, then one day I will bring the whip right up to the box and let the horse investigate it to its heart's content over the half-door. It will sniff at the unfamiliar object and feel the texture with its sensitive mouth, or even make an attempt to play with it. Normally it will lose interest quickly and dismiss it.

Next time I pay a visit, I will bring the whip into the box with me and, having let the horse smell at it, will lean it, standing on end, against the wall in a corner. I then leave it and busy myself with the pitchfork with my back to the horse, which will almost invariably go over to the whip to investigate it thoroughly. It will usually pull at it and throw it over and it will fall obligingly. The horse will start backwards, snort anxiously, arch its neck and take a good look at the thing which is there on the straw, quite harmless and inactive. It will now approach it tentatively and have yet another sniff. The whip, which the horse knew already, smells of me. It is totally harmless. I then go over, pick it up, talk to the horse and gently stroke it along the neck with it. After that I pat the neck, tuck the whip under my arm and leave the box.

When I take the pupil out of the box and lead him to the paddock next day, the whip goes with us, as it will do for a long time to come. It is now accepted in the same manner as the hoof-pick or the dandy brush. The pupil knows all about it and, moreover, it carries my reassuring scent. That is the end of the matter.

Now, while this method is excellent in starting youngsters, it is equally valid when trying to put whip-shy horses right, although in the case of the latter more time will be needed and a great deal more care. Under no circumstances should this work be rushed, the whip should always be held low, i.e. at about hip level, and, as always in handling, the trainer should wait for the moment when the pupil comes of its own accord. One should certainly not force the issue or misjudge the horse's acceptance. Only the horse knows when it has overcome its fear of something, not the tutor, but the animal will be very quick to show the change. As I always say repeatedly; working with horses takes time and patience if a permanent result is to be achieved.

Once the tutor knows the pupil has accepted the passive whip, the moment has come to advance the training to the next step. The tutor begins to teach that the whip is there to direct and to 'tell'. It becomes a means of communication.

I begin by carrying the whip in my left hand when leading. The tip points backwards, and most of the whip is concealed from the animal by my body. I set out at a smart walk and if the horse shows signs of lagging I will touch him lightly on the flank as I say 'Forward' or 'Walk on' at the same instant. He does not really know that the feather-light touch comes from the whip, so he is not frightened by it. If he is young, that light touch on the flank is his first experience of answering to an 'aid'.

Although I will carry the whip in this concealed way for quite a long time, the day will come when the young animal will become accustomed to this gentle aid, and I can change the whip to the leading hand quite openly. The tip will still point back towards the flank, but it will be ready to touch with the mere twist of the wrist as I go along. Somewhere or other along the way the lead rein will be transferred to the left hand to allow freedom to the right, and the horse will be gently stroked from the withers to the base of the tail as we walk along. This will be practised for a number of days until the animal is accustomed to the procedure. The underlying idea behind this apparently complicated approach is to get the horse used to having a whip move over his body in any direction without the need for fear. Indeed, when the horse is fully confident, you should be able to carry the whip tip upwards, as you would a candle.

The final stage that will complete the work presupposes that you have already taught the horse to stand free when told to do so, and is no more than an extension of what has already been described above. If the horse has not yet learned to stand rock steady, then it is taken on the lead rein and stood in the centre of the yard or school, with the tutor standing square in front of it. A piece of carrot is given, and then the tutor begins to stroke the horse very lightly with the whip. He starts at the neck from below the ears to the withers, then from the withers down the shoulder and forelegs, then along the shoulders and as far back along the flanks as the tutor is able to reach. If the animal shows that it likes this treatment, and it usually does, the tutor changes his position to the side of the horse and strokes along the back from withers to root of tail, down the flank behind the deltoid and along the underbelly.

It is well to remember that when standing in front of the horse, you have to cross hands in exchanging the whip, and that this takes place in front of the animal's eyes. If, seeing the whip raised and passed in front of its face does not make it the least nervous, then you may safely say that the pupil is whip-wise.

Should there be any sign of anxiety at any stage, the lesson should be broken off at once, the whip tucked under the arm, the pupil stroked with the hand and then given another piece of carrot. Obviously, the whole exercise will be tried a few weeks later.

There are practically no problems when training a young-ster by this method. Horses that are high in blood and high-couraged are, in my experience, somewhat easier to teach than cross-breds. But regardless of race, any horse that you have handled from the very start will accept what you do with it, and even to it.

You may well ask yourself why all this nonsense, why all this work on what appears to be a detail, when there is so much else to be done? Surely it is unimportant whether the pupil is afraid of the whip or not? The answer is that the whip is by no means unimportant, and that lack of fear of it is very important indeed in the future training and management of the individual.

I have already said that there is practically no phase in the education of one of my pupils in which I do not make use of a dressage whip. I will use it to put pressure on the chest of an impulsive horse that tries to take command when being led; to put pressure on the shoulder of a horse that will insist on swinging in when being led; to touch lightly under the jawbone, if the horse tries to plough the ground with its nose while being led; to keep contact as we walk along; to encourage the hock to become active; and later, as will be seen, it is used in teaching the aids from the ground, before the horse is ever introduced to the saddle or the rider. It will be used extensively when the horse is being worked on long reins or being lunged. It, and the 'touching canes', are the great correctives.

It is for these reasons and many more that the horse must never be allowed to become afraid of any kind of whip. If it is afraid, or even shy, we could never use those fine little touches that are so corrective by their gentle nature, those messages that underline the commands spoken by the voice.

Under such circumstances, it would be folly to hit a pupil. That would be the way to destroy the horse's potential and character and to make it intractable and a devil to handle. I once witnessed a woman diligently lashing the legs and body of a very frightened horse that was refusing to load. I presume that she got it into the trailer eventually and that she scolded all the way home about meddling men and the obstinacy of the animal. It was no good telling her that the horse would be virtually impossible to load in the future, although I suspect it had often experienced similar beatings in the past. Nor would the woman believe that the horse would be whip-shy for life.

I have seen similar irrational behaviour exhibited in various places and in other countries, and it has always been beyond my understanding. The late Dorian Williams[1], writing about the Irish horseman Seamus Hayes, tells us that the latter once said that the surest way of reducing a horse's value from £5000 to £500 within two or three weeks is to indulge in cruelty in its training. This, said Williams, has been Hayes' greatest contribution to show jumping, and one might be tempted to add, horsemanship in general. Although, without wishing to diminish my fellow countryman by the breadth of a hair, Xenophon[2] gave us the same warning a few centuries ago.

Which brings me to the subject of punishment. There are those who talk about punishing a horse. I have come across the word 'punishment' in textbooks as well. It is one thing to give a horse a sharp tap behind the rider's calf, or on the shoulder when riding it, and quite another to belabour it after the event.

Klimke, in a short article on the use of spurs, appearing August 26th, 1983[3], warns against their misuse and suggests that they should not be used by the ordinary rider – the term is mine – but only during competition work as an additional fine aid. He speaks of a light touch and/or 'soft' pressure. The same may be said concerning the use of the whip, except, perhaps, in the heat of the moment when it looks as if a horse may refuse in a difficult situation. But to punish with spurs or lash with the whip in order to 'teach' the horse or make it regret some misdeed, is to show a complete lack of understanding of the animal's nature.

It is a great pitfall to believe that horses understand why they are being hit or punished. The quick application of the whip in a situation when the horse is being ridden, should be no more than what Klimke says the spurs should be, 'the sting of the gnat' which makes the horse start forward.

To believe in punishment, as the human understands it, is to demand human understanding in the horse. This is a sophistication beyond its reasoning powers and cannot even be justified on the grounds that it may be understood by reason of some tradition within equine herd society. A horse will move away from, that is, forward from, the sting of the whip, in order to avoid it. It is much the same reflex as that which prompts a human to get up hastily if he sits on a tin-tack. The horse does not tell itself that it has received the blow because it has failed to do something, or has done something that it should not have done. That would imply rationalisation that is beyond its limited powers of conceptual thought; a recognition of cause and effect. I personally doubt that a rap from the whip on occasion 'A' will influence the animal's behaviour when it is faced with a similar situation 'B', although there are those who postulate the theory that such is the case.

Punishment, which is defined as 'to cause to suffer for an offence', is utterly senseless where animals are concerned, and nothing short of sadism after the event. The concepts of good and evil, of right and wrong, are human abstracts which are beyond equine intellectual capacity. Animals *are* totally innocent. What we like to describe as vices are usually instinctive reflexes and defence mechanisms which, in the case of horses, are often the outcome of irrational handling.

It is therefore morally wrong to inflict punishment of any kind.

To threaten visibly with the whip is to make the horse move away from the whip *per se*, but also from the person who threatens with it and who, as a direct result of his action, then becomes the cause of fright. Under no circumstances will the horse associate the threat or the beating with the cause of it. It *cannot* do so. It is this which makes all punishment of any kind utterly nonsensical.

I am proud to say that my horses come to me when I appear with the dressage whip at the entry to a paddock, all intent on loose schooling them. They know that there is going to be some fun and movement. When we have finished, I will shoulder the whip and walk away and they will mostly follow me.

The mare Tirade appears to distinguish between the dressage whip and the long touching cane, and comes up to me when she sees the latter in the knowledge that there will be a lungeing or driving session. Young Leila, my present pupil, is learning to do the same.

It is rightly so. The whip is merely an extension of the tutor's hand.

References

1. WILLIAMS, DORIAN, *Show Jumping*, Pelham Books, London, 1970.
2. XENOPHON, *Peri Hippikes* (*Über die Reitkunst*, translated by Dr R. Keller), Erich Hoffman Verlag, Heidenheim, 1977.
3. KLIMKE, DR R., 'Sporenhilfe', *Programme Turnier der Sieger*, Verlag Wolfgang Hölker, Münster, 1983.

CHAPTER 14

Walking

WE WOULD DO WELL TO RECOGNISE that walking is the horse's
basic pace, and that it deserves more attention than is usually
paid to it. It is the pace at which muscular resistance is at
its lowest in relation to the vertebral column, which func-
tions as the axis upon which the limbs act to produce movement. Muscular resistance increases at speeds higher than
the walk, to make the spinal column as rigid as possible,
thus eliminating wasteful sideways movements.

Although a horse may cover many miles daily when out
in the paddock, it will only be exercising itself to a limited
extent. This movement is not sufficient to be considered a
basis for training or hard work unless some development is
undertaken. An animal that is constantly out to grass will
be in soft condition and by no means athletic.

In fact, walking in the paddock is not walking at all, in
the sense that I mean. It is a kind of amble with the head
low, looking for grasses and herbs. The walk under such
conditions is not a continuous form of movement, but one
that is interspersed by feeding pauses, the odd gallop and
periods of standing about and looking. Nonetheless, it will

be possible to see the potential quality of the ordinary walk
when the horse moves over a distance of twenty or more
metres and to decide what is required to get it to become a
good mover.

Every phase of teaching and training a young horse over-
laps. The early education concerned with going properly on
the leading rein, parallel leading (see next chapter), standing
and any of the other disciplines taught, all come into play
when we begin to take the pupil for walks with the object
of developing it physically and mentally.

First walks are undertaken inside the paddock in order to
get the animal used to going in-hand for longer periods of
time, because steadiness in-hand is the first requirement if
you are going to walk the pupil as an intregal part of its
training. At first, the handler should not be preoccupied by
anything except forward movement and relaxation. As soon
as you are satisfied that the animal is steady and will do no
more than skitter a bit if something causes it anxiety, you
can take it out for longer walks outside the confines of the
paddock.

It is a wise precaution to carry a dressage whip in your
left hand during the paddock-walking period. The horse
will get used to the idea of it being there. This dressage
whip may later be used to correct, or even to urge the
animal forward if it shows signs of laziness, by tapping it
lightly on the flank just at the point which would be behind
the position of a girth.

Walking is the best method when getting a horse into fit
condition for showing in-hand, breeding or as a preliminary
to any strenuous type of training work. As Neil Dougall
points out in his book[1] on stallion management and handling, 'walking is the traditional British method for getting
a stallion into shape for the breeding season'. The method
cannot be bettered for any type of horse or pony.

I walk young horses a great deal in order to get them fit.
I certainly walk them before I put them to work on the
lunge, because once that stage is reached I will be demanding
quite a lot of them.

Ten minutes' walking should be enough to start with, and the walking time increased over the days and weeks.

To begin with the walk should be long striding and rhythmic, the neck well stretched and swinging as the balancing pendulum, with the horse both physically and, above all, mentally relaxed. If the horse shows any signs of impetuosity do not take it out of the paddock until it is brought under complete control by voice and hand. If the tutor has done the preliminary work well, there should be no question of the pupil behaving in this way when it is brought out walking.

The walking pattern should be varied and the paddock confines used as the means of control. You can then attempt the school figures at walk. Most favoured will be the serpentine, the changes of rein, the diagonal change of rein, the change of rein on the circle, which will make the horse bend and help to bring it under control.

When the horse is walking well in-hand the serious walks may be started. Most horses will become alert and interested once they find out that they are going somewhere with their personal tutor, something that they regard as a treat. At first the pupil may be somewhat slovenly, but this means nothing. The pupil will usually settle down after the first couple of hundred metres and will lighten as it warms up. The head should find its correct position, the tail should come up as the back stretches out and the top-line should alter visibly. The hock should become active. Where all these signs occur, it can be assumed that the pupil is comfortable in itself and that it has found its balance.

The pace is set by the tutor. It should be smart and should aim at covering a minimum of one hundred metres per minute. The handler should walk at the pupil's shoulder and not allow it to lag or fall behind the leading hand. The horse should be talked to and constantly encouraged.

Concentration of effort should be centred on making the pupil walk in a straight line and teaching it to be calm. Whilst a certain amount of phlegm is desirable in competition horses they must be taught to pay attention and walk properly. This does not mean that their fire should be destroyed, or forward movement lost. On the contrary. But we are concerned with achieving a temperament that does not allow itself to be excited by inessentials or by every shadow beyond every tree. The ordinary walk is best developed by allowing little time for the pupil to think about any outside influences, by keeping it on the move.

Walking is no more than extended leading in-hand, at a set pace. Ten minutes means one kilometre or 0.621 of a mile. This would mean five miles in eighty minutes, a reasonably sharp pace.

Where you walk the animal depends upon the surrounding countryside and your liberty to make use of it. This problem does not affect those who have their own land, but some are restricted to the use of neighbours' land, or have permission to walk the rides in woods. Some must use quiet country lanes. Whatever the country to be covered, it is bound to bring its own hazards and excitements where green horses are concerned.

If the tutor is really interested, he should enjoy the walk as much as the pupil does. He watches his charge attentively and talks to it as they go along. All sorts of nonsense is told to it as though it understands every word.

I usually stop for short rest periods in order to allow the pupil to browse for a while. This is a good thing to do. It has the effect of making the horse surer of what is going on. I also make the horse stand quite still from time to time in order to accustom it to the idea of doing so when away from its normal environment. Best results are always achieved in training if variety is introduced to it.

When walking a young horse, the first encounter with a pheasant cock is always an event. The sudden upward explosion from behind a tuft of grass or out of a thicket, the flapping of wings, the cockling voice, loud and indignant at being disturbed, will make the young horse dance in sudden fright. I have experienced five or six such explosions during a single walk. Much consolation and telling the pupil that it is 'all right, all right' will calm it down, as does the fact that the tutor walks on without personal excitement, which is the most reassuring of all.

It is good for the pupil to walk up and down hills, so that it learns to balance itself. The pace is kept as fast as the handler can go, forcing the horse to move on, because it will try to slow down if it can get away with it. In my own area the terrain is mostly flat and any rise in the ground has to be looked for and used. We have a steep little hillock in the grounds and this is used over and over, up one side, down the other, up and down again. The work strengthens the loins and makes the hocks active and the pupil careful of how it puts down its feet.

How to equip the pupil depends upon the animal itself. I have never walked stallions, so do not pretend to know anything about them. I walk mares and youngsters, including colts, naked except for cavesson and lunge rein. I do not use a bit with the cavesson. This will be done when walking with bridle and reins in order to prepare them for showing in-hand. Where this is done, the reins are held in one hand with the off-side rein a fraction shorter than the near-side, but neither so tight as to affect the corners of the mouth.

There should be some slack between hand and mouth with only the weight of the rein restraining. This slack is only taken up when the horse does so. In other words, the pupil is not made to feel the action of the bit unless it pulls against the leading hand. Young horses, not fully accustomed to the bit, should be started on mild vulcanite mullen-mouthed snaffles in order to run no danger of spoiling the sensitivity of the mouth. Later, when the pupil is long reined, the handler will try to educate it to answer to very fine rein aids in the hope that it will respond to them for life.

It is my opinion that a jointed snaffle should not be used until at least six months after the young horse has been backed. This is based on my belief that the jointed snaffle, unless very delicately used, can build up a lot of resistance because of its nutcracker action. For this reason I prefer not

to use a jointed snaffle at all, but opt for a jointed rubber
D-cheek snaffle. Others may disagree, but I can only speak
from my own experience.

When Tirade first went under her young rider, she did so
without the reins being used very much. All work was done
by the rider's back and legs for three months and all that
the animal carried was the weight of the reins in her mouth.
The results were lasting and highly satisfactory.

Young horses may be accustomed to the feel of a girth
by putting on a surcingle for walking. I also use boots in
order to accustom the animal to wearing them.

One should be prepared for resistance, even though the
animal will normally go quietly on the lead rein. First walks
away from familiar surroundings may excite the pupil
beyond all expected measure and it is sometimes difficult to
trace the cause. The unexpected will always happen.

When she was two and a half years old, Tirade could
always be relied upon to spring surprises. Her breeding and
high courage could make her difficult to handle and walks
were sometimes exciting. I took her out on stubble the first
time that she left the grounds. Crossing the public road that
cuts through the estate caused no trouble, nor did the tractors and combine harvester on the land. I led her in a headcollar on the lunge rein, and no more. I chose the moment
because everything was there that might cause trouble when
she came under the saddle. Combines, waggons, tractors,
bales of straw; noise and the unfamiliar combined. She went
like a lamb. The cars and lorries on the road, slightly above
our level, caused her no worry at all.

Next day we went the same route under much the same
conditions. The difference was that she wearing a bridle and
bit, with which she was well familiar. We took the harvested
field first, then a road, followed by a ride through the woods
and back again, a distance of about two miles during which
she fought for her head all the way; a tough and exhausting
walk of a kind that, oddly enough, was never to be repeated.
What got into her that second day will forever remain a
mystery. But she seemed to learn that she could not beat

the leading hand and that was the most valuable thing of all.

One should, if possible, take an experienced horse out with a beginner. The experienced horse will act as school-master and show the young one how to go, and horses learn very quickly from each other, especially if they are paddock friends. But it is not always possible to find somebody who will lead the schoolmaster, or someone who is experienced enough to set the pace. However, if one does get a willing helper, it is best if the green horse is made to follow for at least half a mile before catching up and walking side by side. In difficult or even doubtful situations, the schoolmaster should take the lead at once.

References

1. DOUGALL, NEIL, *Stallions*, J. A. Allen & Co. Ltd, London, 1976.

CHAPTER 15

Parallel Leading and 'Touching'

THIS IS A USEFUL TRAINING METHOD with almost any horse. It establishes control from a distance, corrects faults, allows you to view the gait of the horse and prepares the young or uneducated animal for the lunge. It is also part of my method of progressive teaching, with one phase going over into the next.

Parallel leading is basically nothing more than teaching the horse to work away from its trainer on a relatively taut leading rein. The horse is encouraged to move forward when being led and at the same time taught to walk relaxed and in a straight line.

Every well-treated horse wants to be near to its owner or the person who normally handles it and totally fails to understand that there are times when this is not required. This is the real reason why most horses try to come into the centre of the lungeing circle. They want to be close.

Once I realised this, I decided that, as a horse has to be taught to go straight and quietly when being led, I might as well teach it to walk parallel to me, at a distance, and so lay the early foundations for its conduct on the lungeing rein. I decided to experiment, found that it could be done and used the technique in the teaching of my own animals. It has worked like a charm.

Providing you have the time and the interest, the development of a horse up to the point when it may first be mounted, should be in carefully built up stages. If you wish to have uniform performance, the only way in which to achieve it is to devote time and patience, never to rush anything or to demand too much too soon.

Experience has taught me that the following sequence of education works well with a young horse, or with one that has got to be re-schooled. I have worked out six stages before the animal is ready to be mounted for the first time, which should not be before it is rising four years of age. These stages consist of ordinary leading, walking, parallel leading, introduction to the lunge, lungeing proper and, finally, work on long reins. I call these the stages of movement, as distinct from the six stages of training, which will be discussed in the chapter on lungeing. All other work is undertaken parallel to the stages of movement.

The *leitmotifs* of the movement stages are rhythm and relaxation, without which there can be no true advancement. If the rhythm is wrong and the horse is cramped or anxious, or both, no true progress can be made. It is very important to bear this in mind. There can be no true progress if the pupil is not fully confident of the tutor, or if the same cannot be said of the tutor in relation to the pupil. It is the total transference of mutual confidence and respect which will make the relationship and the work smooth and the horse wholly manageable. Mastery is achieved by trust; problems and problem horses by disunity.

I like to teach parallel leading in a paddock where there is plenty of room, with rails to one side and enough length of ground to allow the horse to walk a straight line.

The horse is led into the paddock and immediately placed between myself and the paddock rail. It is given enough rein to allow me to stretch out an arm and to push it gently away from me through pressure on the shoulder. The rein is then given a little. After that, every time the pupil tries to edge its way towards me, the same little gentle push tells it not to do so. I do a complete circuit of a large paddock, or two of a small one, halt the horse, execute a change of rein and do the whole thing all over again. The first few lessons, which require a fair expenditure of energy on the part of the tutor, are liable to be rather amusing and usually end up with the tutor knowing he has worked and perspiring into the bargain. The next few lessons are usually better. Then, quite unexpectedly, the pupil gets the hang of what is being asked and walks calmly along beside the tutor, but at an arm's length away.

Until this desirable stage is reached, you have to reckon with the pupil's many attempts to come in to you and a great deal of pushing on your part, with the horse swinging its quarters away from you and making contact with the fence. This helps to make it go straight, as well as teaching it to learn its business.

When the teething troubles are a thing of the past and the pupil is accompanying you instead of battling, the moment is at hand to introduce the dressage whip which, from the very start, you have carried in the left hand – or the hand furthest away from the animal – in which you also conduct the lead rein.

The distance between horse and tutor may now be increased by the additional length of the dressage whip, which becomes, as it were, a mere extension of the hand. The whip is used only to preserve distance, either by a gentle touch or a little jab that brings the pupil back onto a straight line.

If you have been careful enough and not confused the pupil, it takes a young horse very little time to understand what is required of it. Spoiled horses may take a bit longer and require more tact and convincing, but they also learn relatively quickly that the tutor is not deserting them when he asks them to walk along beside him, but at some distance away. It goes without saying that the voice plays its part in reassuring the pupil, encouraging it and praising it as it goes along. I normally talk to the pupil, as much to distract its attention from outside influences as to keep its concentration firmly on what we are doing.

When the pupil is used to being directed by the dressage whip, I usually introduce the first of the 'touching canes'. This is carried quite openly in the left hand, or the hand furthest away from the horse, and is pointed towards the sky. The cane is used in the same way as the dressage whip, but being longer it merely increases the distance.

All preliminary work is done within the paddock enclosure. Although this phase is not so interesting for the tutor, it serves the purpose of making the horse walk in a straight line as well as increasing its confidence. However, the preliminary work is accomplished sooner than you realise and you may then attempt the school figures, which are much more interesting. Here the rein is tightened somewhat and tensioned according to the animal's responses, by which I mean that as soon as the horse does what is asked of it, the rein is given, or the tension relaxed.

I begin with ordinary changes of rein for the first lesson. It is important to get these right because the other figures will be influenced by the readiness of the horse to walk straight, keep its distance and respond to the slight pressure of the rein. As soon as I see that the figure is executed with regularity, the counter-change of rein and the diagonal change of rein will follow. Serpentines, the half-volte, the volte and the circle then follow when the horse is responding well. All work is done at the walk. Not only the rein, but the cane as well, will direct and correct the pupil, with the tutor always standing slightly sideways to the animal in order to see exactly how it is performing. The tutor has to walk in a somewhat crablike manner.

There is nothing special about the touching canes. They are cheap to buy and easy to come by, being nothing more than bamboo canes of various lengths, such as may be bought at any garden centre. It is their rigidity that makes them so good for the work. Moreover, you cannot inflict pain with them, even if you were foolish enough to whack the horse in a moment of impatience, which you must never do.

A pupil that has been *trained* to the sight of these canes, may be corrected by their sensible use. The training is the same as that recommended for making a horse whip-wise. The pupil understands that the cane is a means of communication. It would be folly to try touching before the pupil knows what the cane means, and this is especially so in the case of a spoiled or whip-shy horse.

Even a horse that has been trained to them may be made shy if they are not used with restraint. They should never be brandished or waved about. You should do no more than indicate with them, or touch very lightly.

Touching canes are by no means concerned with impulsion alone. The canes may be used to slow down the pupil if it should take it into its head to rush or become impulsive. I will describe the basic touching points most useful to the amateur. They will be remembered by the horse, who will react to them later on when being trained for the lunge.

Ears, crupper and tail should never be touched. The ears because it is unnecessary to do so, the crupper and tail because the horse will cramp, lose stride and rhythm, jam its tail down hard and drop the quarters, all of which is the opposite to what we are trying to achieve. It may be taken as a general rule that it is better to touch too little than too much. The touch should be a *touch*, not a blow and should always be accompanied by a vocal request. The only strong touch that I give at first and until the horse understands the meaning of it, is behind where the girth of the saddle should be. This is done with the tip of the cane and accompanied by the word 'forward'.

These are the touch points and their meaning:

(1) Behind the girth – impulsion.
(2) On the hock – activity and to put the hind feet under.
(3) Under the elbow to the centre of the forearm – to extend and 'lighten' the action of the forelimb.
(4) At the middle of the shoulder, at the middle back of

the deltoid muscle – distance and/or that the pupil straightens its line of progression.

(5) On the chest – to slow down or stop and is linked to the voice command.

The horse is introduced to the cavesson for the first time for this work. The lead rein is attached under the chin, as usual.

The touching points.

CHAPTER 16

Training for the Lunge

A CONSIDERABLE PART of the work with a young horse is
directed towards making it ready for backing. I have said
elsewhere that the more the horse is taken in hand and
the sooner it begins its education, the easier and the more
enjoyable it is to handle and the easier it is to back.

Everything that I have written about so far has been
directly aimed at educating the pupil in such a manner as to
make it an agreeable and tractable companion. At the same
time, no effort has been spared to preserve its spirit and
courage by neither bullying it nor frightening it in any way.
The desire is to have the animal work *with* you and to make
it *understand* whatever you want of it. People who are afraid
of sentimentality and of being accused of 'humanising' their
animals, tend to develop a complex that denies them access
to the realities of an animal's observation powers, its powers
of assessment and its willingness to learn. Because of this,
many fall into the trap of believing that they can only achieve
results by the imposition of mastery of some kind. It has
escaped them that an animal may well enjoy learning, or
being ridden, and is capable of actually looking for direction.

That, by its posture in given situations, it can literally ask the question 'Well, what next?'

It is to our great advantage that young and unspoiled horses seek contact with people and love being handled. Part of the preparatory work involves lungeing. Many riders disdain lungeing in the firm belief that they can exercise their horse better from the saddle, which they probably can, rather than have it 'run round them in a circle'. This is a totally logical and acceptable argument coming from someone who knows little about the discipline and its purpose. Indeed, it is far better that such people remain in the saddle and refrain from spoiling their horse, especially if they cannot but let it *run* around them on the circle, which is certainly the very last thing that one wishes it to do. In most cases they would prefer to get up on it and ride upon its back, for surely, so they argue, that is what they keep a horse for.

Yet the great masters do not scorn lungeing as a discipline. For example, the late Henry Wynmalen[1], Mary Rose[2] and Dr Reiner Klimke[3], to pick out three, each devote a chapter to it in their books, and it is in common usage at the Spanish Riding School in Vienna. While highly reputable institutions like the Westphalian National Stud and the Deutsche Reitund Fahrschule at Warendorf, amongst others, boast a special lungeing hall, it is by no means a new idea, and if we wish to look back, we will see illustrations in early works, as for example those by Johann Elias Ridinger,[4] who shows horses being worked on the lunge. Anybody who dismisses lungeing as a senseless discipline without positive value, should pause and think about it, for it is possible that he has misunderstood its purpose and effect.

Lungeing should not be an exhibition of something resembling a running battle between horse and handler, but this sort of thing is seen quite often, with the animal running in, or stopping, or raising its head and defying its tutor. This may provide entertainment for the spectator, but it is of no benefit, especially in a discipline which should be practised with calm in order to relax and create rhythm. In

169

fact, we can achieve a great deal more on the lunge if we take the time and the trouble to work the pupil properly on the circle and then, when he goes well there and has learned, over cavaletti and obstacles.

The properly lunged horse flexes towards the inside of the circle, walking or trotting smoothly and subsequently with correct impulsion and rhythm. He should watch his handler attentively, responding to the urging and encouragement of the voice with calm concentration. The object of lungeing is not merely to exercise, but to teach and improve.

It is curious that so many amateurs appear not to have learned how to lunge. I must confess I have not yet seen anyone being given a lesson in lungeing at any of the riding clubs I know, although I am prepared to accept that these do take place. Nor have I ever heard any theoretical discussion on the subject. Perhaps I am over-critical, but it seems to me that if lungeing has been taught, the lessons cannot have been of any great benefit.

I used to be a purist when it came to lungeing technique and was filled with an ardent desire to lunge 'correctly'. I followed the methods advocated in text books, or those used by experts, whom I considered to be of a standard far and away above myself.

I gave the matter a great deal of thought and the logical conclusion I reached was that the animal must be *taught* to go on the lunge, just as it must be taught everything else. At the same time, however, it became clear to me that the teaching should be done before the pupil is introduced to the circle, cavesson and long reins. Although this would take time and care, it would be more profitable than wasting time trying to get the horse right after I had confused it by asking it to accept something that it might have difficulty in understanding.

If you read the text books carefully, they invariably state that a horse cannot be taught without the aid of an assistant. This apparently quite invaluable individual walks the outside of the circle at the head of the pupil, steadying it and making it move forward, while the tutor places himself in the centre of the circle to become the pivot around which the animal is expected to move on the rein. Much depending upon the tutor, but at a slightly more advanced stage, the assistant will continue to urge the horse forward by following it with the lungeing whip, unless the teacher prefers to take the whip in his own hands.

The theory is possibly admirable, but it means that somebody like myself who starts and works his very green horses alone, would either have to hire an assistant, or rely upon the services of one of the family or a kind friend. Should none of these be available, the only alternative would be not to lunge the horse at all.

I will tolerate no assistant, no member of the family, no kind friend at the start, and most certainly no 'whip man'. If the horse is to go properly, nobody will be asked to assist and confuse and upset the concentration of teacher or pupil. In short, lungeing is an intimate and private affair, and, I repeat, in no way should the pupil be put out on the circle and be expected to know what to do instinctively and without previous training. If one has followed the suggestions which I have made so far, lungeing is an extension of all that the pupil has learned.

Lungeing is just as important a part of equestrianism as accomplishment in the saddle. To lunge, and to lunge with an eye, soon reveals what the horse is doing wrong, and is a valuable aid in showing what must be attended to by the rider.

Of course, if one merely wishes to exercise the horse without putting it under the saddle, one may have recourse to the lunge, but ideally, one lunges, or ought to do so, for the wholly different purpose of schooling.

It will be remembered that when the horse was learning to go properly on the leading rein and refused to do so, I recommended that the handler made it circle him instead. The pupil was forced to continue circling, long after it had put up its resistance to its master's will, and then led forward when the handler thought that it had had enough. Although no great issue was made of it, those were the first lessons

171

in lungeing. Later, when touching with the canes in parallel leading, the handler extended the length of the leading rein and kept the pupil away by touching it at the shoulder, and making it circle, so that the handler could look at its movement from a little distance. That was the second indirect lesson in lungeing.

On these circles the pupil was forced to bend, or flex, and had to balance himself carefully. Because of its lateral stiffness, however, the pupil did not, as one might have thought, bend its body in order to master the curve that it was being forced to follow, but had to roll somewhat in that cradle of muscle that suspends the thorax between the forelimbs. (This is explained in greater detail in the next chapter.)

If you think about the school figures when teaching, it takes little imagination to see that nearly all of them are designed in one way or another to make the horse flexible and to bend laterally, thus forcing it to take a course that it would not normally follow in freedom. They demand a physical effort that is strenuous and requires concentration. Lungeing is a preliminary to this work which has already been started in parallel leading where the same school figures were practised, with this difference: that not until the horse is being lunged will it really be working with consistent and regular rhythm.

I cannot see the virtue of the tutor standing in the centre of the circle, unless he is training the pupil as a vaulting horse. But even were I doing so, I should first work with any horse by my method, which is to move with it. By moving with it, I get the horse to move forward. The pupil is *watching* me all the time, which means that if I move, it will do so as well. I stand slightly sideways to the motion so I may continually watch the horse's performance and correct with the touching cane. Mathematically, my field of movement is relatively small and is determined by the length of the cane in my hand, so that by extension, I am really parallel leading, which is something that my pupil already understands.

The first lessons, which will not be more than five or, at the most, ten minutes' duration, will be alone with the pupil and at walk. We will walk the circle together, chatting, and preventing any inclination to walk into or out of the circle by means of the touching cane or dressage whip in my hand. What I do, in fact, is to extend the experience of parallel walking, so I do not put on the breaking cavesson, nor use the lungeing rein, but work with headcollar and a 13-foot leading rein. The cane or whip will determine the distance between myself and the horse.

When I have walked the circle a couple of times, I make the pupil stand for a few seconds, then change the rein and start all over again. You can, if desired, trot the horse on the circle, then bring it back to the walk and stop, but I prefer to work at walk, until the pupil begins to show signs of really understanding what is going on. By way of a change, because I am always trying to keep the animal's interest, I do a half circuit of the circle and walk out of it, still preserving the set distance from the animal's shoulder, still walking parallel to it all the time, just as I did when correcting its walk during earlier exercises. After that, back to the circle, a couple of rounds, and that is enough for the first lesson. A pat, then a reward, and home.

I follow the same procedure during the next few lessons, but at each lesson I increase the distance between myself and the pupil and I lengthen the touching canes. The horse finds the work strange, even uncomfortable, because it wants to come in to its tutor, but whenever it tries to do so I give it a little prod on the shoulder which reminds it to keep its distance, and because I am continually talking and soothing, it becomes accustomed to staying away from me. If it should show signs of slowing down, a tickle just where the girth should be, helps to urge it forward and a touch on the hock will remind it that I want to have the latter active and put well under.

When I consider the pupil confident enough, because it goes so well and so steadily on the 13-foot rein, I introduce the breaking cavesson and the long lungeing rein. While the horse is still kept only 13 feet away from me, I begin to teach it what I will be asking of it with voice and gesture. The aids that I teach will be the signals which tell it to walk, trot, canter, and stop, and it will be my aim that when the pupil is really advanced, all I shall have to do is to point with the index finger of the free hand in order to emphasise what my voice is asking.

Right from the start, the pupil should be taught the vocabulary that will be used in lungeing. The human voice is one of the most important tools or aids during the work. I use 'forward' or 'walk on', 'steady', 'quiet', 'slow', 'watch your head', 'take care', or simply a sharply uttered 'Eh!' for indiscipline, 'slow' and 'stand' or 'Br–r–rh' to make the horse stop. Also, 'good boy', 'there's my girl' or any other sentence that you wish to use as a means of praising. The voice is always calm and low keyed. It is unnecessary to raise it, because horses have extremely sharp hearing and a shouting voice not only hurts them, but does not coordinate with a quiet hand.

I use a touching cane because I am moving with the pupil. I have given up making use of a whip because the cane will tell the horse all that it has to know, so several cane positions are taught and are memorised by the pupil. Thus, the cane pointed at the shoulder means walk; the cane pointed at the hind quarters at about the level of the hock means trot; the cane pointed at the head means watch your head; and the cane held parallel to the ground, but pointing towards the chest of the horse, means slow down, walk or stop, depending upon the voice command. The cane held with the point to the sky and in the left hand means everything is all right. These signals are always supported by the use of the tutor's voice and are quickly learned by most reasonably intelligent horses and ponies.

The cane is also used to touch the pupil. A tap on the hock means pick up your feet and put the hock under. A tap on the flank, just behind the girth, asks for impulsion. A tap, or even a poke, on the shoulder means don't run in. If the horse will not obey the command to slow down, walk or stop, as the case may be, the tutor takes a step in its direction, takes up an appropriate amount of rein, draws the head slightly in towards the centre, re-issues the demand and presses against the pupil's chest with the cane. Unless the pupil is very impulsive or excited, this will usually have the desired effect.

When the young animal obeys the signals, walks and trots well on the circle and goes in a presentable straight line in a calm manner, the time has come to bring it onto the circle and begin lungeing proper.

Some horsey people are disturbed when they see me walking the circle with the horse, albeit 13 feet away from it. They are always at great pains to tell me that I am doing it wrong. I agree I am not working in the classic manner, which is about as far as I will go. From my point of view, such criticism is somewhat hidebound by lack of imagination and a trifle too much conservatism, especially so because it is almost invariably levelled without enquiring *why* I work in this way.

Let me therefore explain the logic at this point. By moving with the young and inexperienced horse, or one that has been spoiled and is constantly interrupting the work by putting up defences, you encourage the animal to move forward. By placing yourself slightly behind the shoulder you therefore drive the pupil ahead of you, so demanding forward movement. I do not use the term impulsion at this stage. In moving with the pupil, you make it confident that you are not deserting it and show that what you are demanding is done in conjunction with yourself. You actually work with the pupil. In addition, you are in a good position to set pace and rhythm as you go along.

I always console my critics by telling them that the day will come when I lunge the horse from the centre of the circle in the way that everybody likes, and thinks right. But not when the horse is a raw beginner, and not when I want to correct it by touching when it is on the lunge.

The effect of the preliminary work, what you should be looking for and why, will be fully discussed in the following chapter.

References

1. WYNMALEN, HENRY, *Equitation*, J. A. Allen & Co. Ltd, London, 1971.
2. ROSE, MARY, *Training Your Own Horse*, George Harrap & Co. Ltd, London, 1977.
3. KLIMKE, DR R., *Cavaletti*, J. A. Allen & Co. Ltd, London, 1969.
4. RIDINGER, J. E., *Schul– und Campagne Pferde* (1760), Die bibliophilen Taschenbücher, Harenberg Kommunikation, Dortmund, 1978.

CHAPTER 17

Lungeing

I LIKE TO LOOSE-SCHOOL THE PUPIL before taking it on the lunge. A horse that has been confined to its box for a day or two, or that has not been worked for a while, may either be so peppery that it is difficult to handle quietly, or so lazy that it doesn't really begin to wake up to the latent strength and go in its body until it has moved a bit.

I chase the horses first, using a schoolmaster and an inexperienced youngster, who will copy what the experienced horse is doing. This is great fun and is usually accompanied by much kicking up of the heels, wild galloping and then trotting, when the horses have got rid of the high spirits and replaced them with the full beauty of an unrestricted and elevated trot. When this happens, they are ready for loose-schooling proper and will circle the handler of their own volition, keeping a distance of about fifteen yards from where I stand at the centre of affairs, calling for the pace I want. A couple of minutes of this and one or other of the horses will be called to me and taken away to the circle.

Recognised lungeing equipment consists of seven items, which are listed overleaf:

(1) the surcingle,
(2) the breaking cavesson,
(3) the bridle, but without noseband,
(4) side reins,
(5) the lungeing rein,
(6) the lungeing whip,
(7) bandages.

I am fully aware of other people's ideas as to how a horse should be worked on the lunge, and I do not intend to discuss what I consider to be the merits and faults of them here. Everybody working seriously has his own theories and competence, to some extent, while adhering in principle to the generally accepted rules of experience. I, for example, am greatly influenced by Wynmalen[1] and Becher[2] whose approach and, above all, thinking, appeal to me.

However, because I work alone, I have found it necessary to evolve my own methods from the theories and practice of others, developing them, by constant practice, into what suits me best. My whole method of educating the horse from the moment it comes into my hands, is to produce a mannerly and reliable animal with which to begin. It has to behave so well in-hand as to allow me to practise my own deviations linked to the use of the voice. If I have not taken the trouble to develop such an animal, neither my theories, nor those of anybody else, are of any great use. You have to understand the individual animal which then works with you as a partner.

It is for this reason that I dispense with the surcingle, the bridle, the side reins and the lungeing whip, replacing the latter with a long fibreglass touching cane. Before there is an outcry of 'all wrong', remember that the pupil has been very painstakingly prepared and conditioned to work quietly. Even very high-couraged and high-spirited animals will work in a businesslike manner if taken early in-hand and taught to obey the disciplines. The contact felt through the lungeing rein should be sufficient to establish control because of the close personal relationship we are always hearing and reading about, but which we are so seldom privileged to see.

It is the *leitmotif* of this book that the personal relationship between horse and tutor, or horse and rider, quite apart from the techniques which are most effectively achieved through it, is the alpha and omega of equestrianism and handling.

I do not use the surcingle until I reach a reasonably advanced stage of driving the horse on long reins, because I will use a saddle instead when engaging in what is known in Continental Europe as 'double lungeing', which is really the first stage of work on long reins.

Side reins are not used because they defeat the object of the exercise. You want the head and neck to be stretched forward, just as you wish to harmonise the movement of the long muscle of the back, *longissimus dorsi*, in order to co-ordinate all the muscle groups. Therefore it is pointless to tie the horse up. If you do not restrict with the side reins but keep them loose, they serve no purpose. You may as well save yourself the bother of having them there at all. The only meaningful side reins are those which are crossed in front of the chest and restrict, to some extent, the lateral flexion of the head and neck; or running reins attached near the saddle pommel, drawn between the front legs and attached under the girth. They permit the horse a certain amount of stretch if properly adjusted, but I do not approve of them during the initial stages; only later, when some collection is demanded.

Following Wynmalen's reasoning that side reins defeat the purpose of lungeing because they interfere with the lateral bend and free use of the neck and head as a balancing pendulum, I redesigned and remade our cavesson to allow the lunge to be attached under the chin, totally removing the nose dee, and altered the chin strap to take a dee to which the billet may be attached. This means that the horse is about six inches ahead of the hand when lungeing, which I consider to be an advantage all round. In addition, the weight of the lunge rein is carried by the head from under the chin and does not press on the nose, which is more comfortable for the horse. The animal may stretch, move laterally and find its balance through the pendulum action of head and neck.

The main object at all times is to produce a *relaxed* and confident horse that will ultimately go lightly on the bit, that feels no need to put up defences, that can be quietened down by the mere sound of your voice should it become frightened or excited, that works with you and not against you. At the same time, you wish to teach the horse to go forward very willingly, and you want to improve the carriage of the head. You want to make the pupil walk freely, and to eliminate any stiffness. But above all, you want the pupil to learn to bring his hind legs under him – to activate the hock – to make use of his head and neck as a pendulum, and to balance himself, flex the ribs and supple himself laterally.

It is useless to approach any of these things without having some elementary idea of a horse's anatomical structure, of its lateral stiffness, of the relative rigidity of the spine, or of the function of the main muscles and how they work in relation to the horse's capability of movement, or why the 'engine' of the horse is at the back and that almost all forward movement comes from there. You must also understand that the horse is capable of moving not only forward, but also sideways at the same time. You must know that the front legs are not attached to the spine – the horse has no clavicle – the front legs being held in place by those muscles which form what is known as the *thoracic sling*. It is this construction that allows the horse to round bends by raising the inner leg and dropping the outer one, a process known as abduction and adduction. By adducting one forelimb and abducting the opposite limb, the horse, when bending around a corner, actually rolls in the thoracic sling. Because of this cradling of the thorax, the horse, as I have already said, is able to move both forwards and sideways at the same time, with both limbs moving at the same speed, but with the outer one taking the stronger stride.[3] An extreme example of this may be seen in the American quarter horse during barrel racing, where the animal keels over at such an angle to the ground that you wonder why it does not fall.

The above information is the least that you should know when approaching the lungeing of a horse if you do not wish to damage it by demanding too much and consequently straining or overtaxing muscles.

Work in a circle requires real effort, and obviously the tighter the circle, the more strain is put upon the horse. It is therefore hoped that by the time you have worked with an animal for some months, the lateral stiffness will have decreased, because the pupil has suppled up, and you will be able to lead it in quite tight circles without its cramping and resisting. Lungeing is the number one corrective work as well as being the most complete of exercises.

Every horse has a stiff side, which becomes noticeable during work. The horse does not want to work on that side because bending causes it discomfort. Generally, the defence that is put up is an attempt to come in and change rein. Care should therefore be taken to supple up this side. This may be done by bending the horse around you, shortening the rein so that you decrease the circle to about 16 feet in diameter. Once every now and again is enough, at random, about once a week. You should not overdo close bending as it is hard on the animal's legs, and you should not allow more than half a minute or a minute for this work. If the horse is reasonably accomplished on the lunge, or later, when being worked on long reins, it is no harm to make it move on its stiff side for a little longer than on its more flexible one. But you must avoid causing it distress.

In the previous chapter, which dealt with training the horse for the lunge, I made mention of what I describe as the classical method of approaching this work, and I believe that this is a good point at which to discuss classicism in the discipline.

The classical and, incidentally, correct method used at the beginning of a lungeing session, is to introduce the horse to the circle, lead it around it for some distance, even a full round, and then, walking backwards away from it so that you face the moving horse, spiral your way into the centre of the circle, giving rein as you go. This is the moment when the rein is adjusted and freed of any twists, and the surplus neatly looped to hang free from the lungeing hand. The rein to the horse should be flat and, if my way of lungeing is adopted, passed through the third and fourth fingers of the lungeing hand.

The lungeing hand is that hand whose shoulder follows the direction of the horse's head. The whip hand is that hand that faces the quarters. Thus, if the horse is moving to the left, the right hand faces the quarters.

This method of placing the horse on the circle and the positioning of the handler described, should be followed when the horse has been taught the business, but should not be attempted before it. The textbook method of introducing the young horse to the lunge is to have an assistant lead the horse around the circle on the outside, so steadying it and giving it confidence until it learns what to do. This individual may then be entrusted with the whip in order to encourage the horse to go forward. It is theoretically a splendid idea, were it not for the fact that the green or even nervous animal must concentrate its attention on *two* people, and many a horse has become nervous and even frightened of the lunge for just this reason. As I have said, I do not believe in having the animal shadowed by anyone with a whip in his hand, and I do not believe in an assistant leading it round the circle. I repeat, lungeing is an intimate affair.

No less important than getting the pupil right is the personal conduct of the tutor in the circle regardless of whether he is moving with the pupil or conducting the training from the circle's centre. When riding, the rider should be as concentrated as the horse, and lunge work is no different. All of us have seen the unconcentrated person holding the lunge, the sloppy stance, the roving eye, the twisted, hanging rein, the complete lack of true contact, the whip that is cracked or that trails on the ground.

The tutor should be alert and concentrated, his eyes for the horse only. This is the moment when any necessary corrections should be made between hand and horse. The rein should have a slight belly in it, the amount of slack between hand and head nicely adjusted at the same time, for the slack will be taken up when corrections are being made and will allow for the constant giving and taking of the rein, as in riding. The animal must be comfortable in itself and able to find its balance naturally. The tutor should not want to pull it around the circle by means of the rein, nor it to pull the tutor. The lungeing hand should be sure and firm. If a whip is used, the lash should be run out out with skill – it requires some practice – and should do no more than tickle the horse. If a touching cane is used, it should be pointed. In either case, the demand should be vocal as well. Lungeing sessions are vocal affairs, not dumb shows, but the voice should be gentle and calm. One cannot expect calm relaxation if you are not prepared to radiate it, nor interest if you are not prepared to show it yourself. This cannot be over-emphasised.

The primary rhythm is developed at walk, the ordinary walk being the pace selected. This pace demands a strong, diligent, ground-covering and relaxed movement, in which the action of the hind hoof brings it into the print left by the forefoot. The ordinary walk is in four time, each separate hoof striking the ground distinctly and in uniform sequence. This is what you are looking for and concentrating on achieving. However, you are also looking for relaxation, because without it there will be no uniformity. A horse which is anxious or nervous, or both, and which cannot be reassured by the tutor's voice at all times, will break its rhythm and become ragged and uncertain in its movement, cramped, tense and excited.

I therefore concentrate on rhythm and on straightening the spine. The horse must be taught to fit the long axis of its body to the track, regardless of whether this is straight or curved or circular. Success is recognised when the imprint of the front hoof will be covered by that of the rear one.

Any outward deviation of the rear hoof is faulty because it signifies that the hind quarter is no longer developing impulsion exactly in the gravitational line and that the axis is not straight. This has to be corrected at once. I do this by asking for a change of hand, which is a total break in the rhythm, since it involves the horse standing in the track, being turned, and re-starting the movement in the opposite direction. If this works, then there will be another change of hand after a couple of rounds. If it doesn't work at all, the lunge line will be shortened and the animal parallel-led on the track. If that does not work, one leads the horse off the track and parallel-leads it in a straight line when one may correct the apparent fault by delicate touching. This is one occasion when I normally use an assistant to lead the animal away from me and follow it with a touching cane in my hand. I may then observe not only the movement of the horse, but the imprint of the hooves as well.

The ordinary trot comes next. It should always be regular and vigorous. The striking of the hooves should be heard as two regular beats, if the two pairs of diagonal legs are working properly. It is this regularity, coupled with active movement in a straight line, that is being looked for. It is pointless trying to advance the work until you have reached near perfection of performance in these two paces, because unless you concentrate on them at first, the horse will go to pieces when it is ridden.

I lunge on a permanent circle with a diameter of 30 feet. It is outdoors and confined by a fence on two of its 'sides' and by water on another. Twelve years of lungeing on it have deepened it and it is filled with turf. The open sides, that which is near the water and that which faces the paddock, are furnished with clatter boards. This circle is only used for slow paces. If a horse is cantered, it will be cantered elsewhere and at the full length of the lunge.

I do not ask for a canter until the pupil is quite experienced at the work. I have found that if you canter a young horse too soon, much of what you have taught it in the way of discipline may, depending upon the temperament of the individual, be undone very quickly. Young animals tend to become excited at this pace and try to get their heads and to break out and away from the hand with their quarters. This is because their concentration goes or becomes upset. An experienced horse will seldom react so. Horses that are unable to support themselves will change over to a trot, and when you see that this is about to happen, you should immediately ask for a trot and so prevent the pupil from dictating the pace even though you know perfectly well that he is not doing so. I therefore only canter horses on a lunge when I have plenty of space and the animal is in good condition, preferring to get the strong paces out of him during loose schooling. However, if the horse is in first-class form, I will be able to canter him with restraint and so control him as to make the rhythm right and the pace regular.

Constant working with a horse will enable you to regulate the tempo from your place within the circle. Tempo is regulated by a rein aid, the voice and an indication of the whip or hand. If the pace is to be slowed, the rein is tightened and the horse drawn slightly towards the centre of the circle, told to slow as the touching cane is passed forward horizontally over the rein to point ahead of the animal's chest. As soon as the pupil responds, the rein is given by the amount it was taken up, the horse praised and the cane returned to the vertical. If the tempo is to be increased, a fraction more rein is given, the horse told to go forward and the cane pointed at the middle of the barrel.

Incidentally, I train the horses to the word 'forward' instead of 'come'. Many trainers recommend the latter word, but I cannot use it as my animals are trained to come to hand if I say 'come', so to use it while lungeing would be to invite them to join me at the centre of the circle.

When the hindlegs are showing plenty of thrust accompanied by a stretching of the body, the animal may be taken to be relaxed, giving an indication that it would be coming up on the bit. As soon as the hindlegs are stretching nicely and bending well, one knows that the horse is distributing the carrying of its load properly. At the same time, the back will be showing some bend and the head and tail will be in a good position. The step will become springy and light, showing that the joints of the hindlegs are elastic and functioning as they should.

When the training is advanced and the horse showing proficiency, side reins may be introduced with the purpose of supporting the clean, vigorous gait. The outer rein is adjusted somewhat shorter than the inner one which, in the case of crossed reins, means that the adjustment is made on the nearside. The better the horse becomes at its work, the more the reins may be taken up. I personally do not use this method because as soon as the animal is going as I want it to go, I will switch over to double lungeing, which I consider to be better, because I will be able to get what I want directly with my hands.

Cavaletti work and jumping may be started when the pupil is steady and straight. Here the adjustment of the lunge rein in its contact between head and hand becomes a matter of major importance. The amount of slack should be no more than may be taken up by a quick twist of the wrist. One gives more rein, or takes it in, by a movement of the elbow. For cavaletti work, the hand is held on a level with the waist. If I am asking the horse to jump, I will raise my hand to the level of mid-chest. This may not be approved, but I find it effective because the lunge line will help the horse carry its head and allow it to come down on the rein without danger of entanglement.

As usual, I move with the horse which is first made to trot evenly and then made to change track in order to place it in line with the obstacle. Some rein is given at the precise moment that the horse is stretching out to take the jump, and then quickly taken up again when it has cleared. It needs a little practice. You can either place the obstacles in a circle, or in a straight line if you are prepared to run with the pupil as you must if you have a double jump, or a series of them.

Equipment is confined to the lunge rein, the cavesson, a surcingle with an unbacked horse, or a saddle without stirrups, boots and leg bandages. No side reins. The horse must be able to find itself and to stretch. There is no bit, because of the danger of jerking the pupil in the mouth. I am looking for balance.

Long wing poles angled from the ground to the top of the fence or obstacle are a must in the interest of safety. They will prevent the rein catching at the top of the fence when the horse is approaching and clearing it. Lack of skill in the manipulation of the rein might cause the horse to crash into the jump and lead to nasty accidents.

Fences should be low at first, the height being gradually increased as the pupil becomes more familiar with the work. Even when the animal has become more proficient, you should not become ambitious and look for too much height. Far better to look for accuracy of the hindquarters and calmness because these are more important. Jumping lessons should, in my opinion, not be something very special, but introduced during the course of a week as a change of routine, as a part of the lungeing session, and neither their frequency nor length should be overdone. I imagine that too long sessions at jumping even small obstacles may tempt a pupil to rush the fences, but I have not had any experience of this to date.

Spreads should be included in the routine when the pupil shows general proficiency. This may sound vague, but the fact of the matter is that only the tutor can judge what he would describe as proficiency, because the degree will depend upon his knowledge of the horse's capability and individuality. Some horses show great talent and learn very quickly, some are reluctant, lazy or slow, and others are unwilling, so that the amount of time required to make them do what one wishes will naturally vary. Remember not to rush or force them or to overdo the work. It is always better to take a little more time than to advance too quickly in spite of the fact that the pupil may seem to know it all. Lessons should stick for life.

Some horses really enjoy jumping, but not all of them do. However, those with the spirit and the talent for it should be encouraged. When they are taking their spreads nicely, solid-looking jumps may be offered to them. I like to use straw bales with a white pole on top of them. I use about four bales placed end to end for this. Later on, a second row will be put on top of them with a pole laid in front as well. Although there is no danger of a young animal damaging itself when these are used, you must still insist on angled wing poles for the lunge.

I believe that if you approach lungeing seriously with the aims outlined in this and the foregoing chapter in mind, then it may hardly be argued that in lungeing, one is asking the pupil to 'run' around one in a circle. Nor can it be said that one is lungeing merely to exercise the horse. In teaching the animal to be calm and relaxed, to fit its long axis to the track and so walk in a straight line, to develop the consistency of walk and trot, you are demanding fundamental correctness that is as applicable to a horse that has been spoiled and must therefore be reschooled, as much as to a green young beginner.

I do not even try to ask for any sort of collection on the lunge. I will ask for it very, very much later on in long reins when the horse has already been under the rider. By that time it will have learned the diagonal aids on long reins, as well as becoming bridle wise.

In conclusion, let me sum up the points that we wish to achieve when lungeing:

(1) Total calm and relaxation of the pupil.
(2) Strengthening and development of all the muscles.
(3) Improvement of lateral flexion.
(4) Improvement of balance, therefore of head carriage.
(5) Relaxation of the neck.
(6) Development and improvement of walk and trot in a straight line.
(7) Development of consistent rhythm.
(8) Development of forward movement, impulsion.

(9)   Strengthening of the back.
(10) Improvement in the flexion of the stiff side.
(11) Development of consistent obedience to voice, whip and touching cane signals.
(12) Elementary cavaletti work.
(13) Elementary jumping.
(14) General correction of faults.

References

1.   WYNMALEN, HENRY, *Equitation*, J.A. Allen & Co. Ltd, London, 1971.
2.   BECHER, ROLF, *Erfolg mit Longe, Hilfszügel und Gebiss*, Erich Hoffmann Verlag, Heidenheim, 1970.
3.   SMYTHE, R. H. and GOODY, P.C., *The Horse*, J. A. Allen & Co. Ltd, London, 1973.

CHAPTER 18

Long Reining and First Lessons in the Aids

SCHOOLS OF THOUGHT in relation to long reining vary; there are some who maintain footwork of this kind is not necessary and even a waste of time because all may be taught from the saddle; a point which I have already discussed in the chapter on lungeing. Then there are others who, like myself, argue that you cannot very well teach a horse which is too young to come under the saddle, anything from the saddle. I maintain that a horse should not be mounted until it is rising four or, better still, over four years of age, but at the same time I believe in muscular development of the legs and back. This is unquestionably the ideal way of doing the preliminary work, with the added advantage that, when the youngster is being brought forward by a tutor who is on foot, all its movements and defects may be assessed and relatively easily remedied.

In long reining, as with lungeing, the true value of the work must be dependent upon the tutor's understanding of what he is doing and aims to achieve. The sequence of preparation, beginning with plain in-hand leading, parallel leading and lungeing, has, as its objective, the well-mannered and potentially reliable riding horse, whether it is merely intended for pleasure riding or high-grade show events. Not only has the horse been shown and taught what is expected of it, but it has also learned to respond to the touch, as well as the voice, as a means of communication and control. It is therefore logical to follow up ordinary lungeing by 'double lungeing' and then by simple driving on long reins.

Although there is little difference between 'double lungeing', as it is called in Europe, and work on long reins, I use both terms here in order to clarify the two steps. The difference is a matter of definition of the tutor's position in relation to the horse, as well as the handling and position of the reins. The pupil must have already been made familiar with the weight and feel of a saddle on its back, or at least with rollers with large rings, and a snaffle bridle if one is to be used. In double lungeing, the off-side rein is passed from the bit or cavesson through a stirrup or ring, along the body of the horse and brought to the near-side over the hock to the tutor's hand, while the near-side rein is equally carried by a stirrup or through a ring attached to a roller, thence to the tutor's hand. The tutor takes up his position about level with the end of the animal's rib cage, and operates from there.

When long reining, the tutor works from behind the pupil with the reins passed through the stirrups or rings directly to his hands, neither rein passing over the hock. The tutor therefore drives the horse forward, and will change his own position according to need. Experience in rein manipulation will eventually allow the saddle or the roller with rings to be disposed of, the tutor working close up to the horse.

Many people avoid this kind of work because they are afraid of the damage that they might do to the horse's mouth; although that is something that may easily be averted. It is a very good way to train a green horse that is to be ridden, to respond to the rein aids, and further lessons, when it is far enough advanced to allow direct driving on long reins, will give the tutor the opportunity to condition the pupil to accept the leg aids. Indeed, as the training advances, it is possible to teach the horse to respond to leg and rein aids and to accustom it to the time pause between the application of the two.

Further advantages that may be reaped, are that the young animal will learn to move forward when urged from behind, as well as to associate the feel of the saddle in combination with the weight of the reins carried by its mouth. In addition to developing its tendons and muscles, the pupil will also learn obedience, steadiness and self-control.

A pupil that has learned to go steadily on the lunge and that works well and trustingly with its tutor, gives little trouble when it is first introduced to the double lunge. Although it may at first cramp up and press down its tail, or overbend, it will soon understand what is being asked of it and go nicely when it has learned to accept the bridle and subsequently to flex.

It is true that the trainer must be careful not to end up by making a hardmouthed animal instead of one that is very fine and responsive to the rein aids, but a youngster can be spoiled no less effectively when first going under a rider.

However, there is no reason at all to be beset by fears, because both horse and tutor can get along without the use of a bit if they are learning the business together. The obvious way of avoiding trouble and of having one's cake and eating it, is to attach the reins to the side dee rings of a breaking cavesson. Then even if the hands are a bit inept in the manipulation of the reins, no damage can be done. The worst effect that hard hands could produce in this case, would be a hackamore restraint on the pupil's nasal bone.

While we are on the subject of hands, it might be good to recite Wynmalen's[1] definition of them. 'Good hands are hands that need rely on no greater strength than that of the *fingers*, that are consequently "light" and know how to give and take; they should be able, when required, to give when the horse gives and to take when the horse takes: they should, ultimately, be able to maintain contact by the *weight* of the reins alone.' The emphasis is mine.

I prefer to use a breaking cavesson during the initial stages of teaching, partly because the horse is already accustomed to it from lungeing and therefore feels at home, and partly because it prevents any tearing at the mouth before the horse is used to the new discipline.

Concentration of effort is directed towards the pupil being taught to understand that the reins will dictate the direction in which it is to move, by telling it through a light pressure on the appropriate rein. This will be its first experience of direct rein aids, and you should remember while teaching that this will be the only phase of its education in which it will have to answer such direct rein aids because much later, when you teach it to respond to the leg aids, you will begin at once with diagonal aids.

I had a saddler make my long reins to suit my own requirements. We chose webbing as a suitable material. It is tough, cheap, washable and does not slip in wet hands. The reins are 16 feet long and ¾-inch wide. They are fitted with ¾-inch wide leather straps furnished with suitable buckles. These allow for quick and easy attachment to the dee rings of the cavesson, or to the snaffle rings. They may be joined together by a buckle and strap, as in ordinary reins. It is advisable not to join them when double lungeing, although I do so when long reining. Many trainers use two standard lungeing reins, but I find them too long and diffi-cult to manipulate. The surplus length always seems to drag out along the ground behind me, all out of control.

It must be said here that work on long reins requires tact and patience, as well as a good feeling for the pupil. Interest is a prerequisite to success. If the would-be tutor cannot command these assets, then he would be wise to give up the idea and stick to lungeing with a single rein.

Should the tutor lack confidence the first few times that he attempts working with his pupil, it is no harm to have an assistant in case the horse springs forward, or becomes frightened by the novelty of the experience.

I work alone, partly because I have not always somebody to help me, but mainly because, as I have already said, such training is a personal matter between the horse and myself. I never go out with the pupil on those days when I know that I am upset or irritable, because the vibration is picked up through the reins and the pupil is almost certain to become upset.

I like to prepare the pupil long before I take it out for the first time, by introducing it to the feel of the long reins. The passage of the outside rein over the hindleg above the hock may very well cause discomfort, tickle, irritate or even frighten an animal not accustomed to it, and it is this rather than anything else that the horse has to learn to accept. So, for a week or two before beginning serious work, the pupil is given some easy lessons designed to prevent it becoming excited when it first experiences the manipulation of the rein over the hock.

What I do is as follows. I put on the breaking cavesson, tether the animal to the hitching rail by attaching the tether under the chin and then put on the saddle, with which the pupil is already familiar. The stirrups are then lengthened to a position about 8 inches above the pupil's elbows and secured to each other with a length of strong cord, tied to each stirrup with a slip knot for easy release. This is passed dead centre of the girth, so that the wearer only has the pressure of the girth to contend with. This cord will be replaced when serious work begins, by a leather strap, about 4 feet long, passed around the horse in exactly the same manner.

When this has been done, the reins are slipped through the stirrups first and then attached to the dee rings of the cavesson, or if one is making use of one, of the snaffle. The horse is prepared for the first dummy run. The off-side rein is slid gently down over the crupper and brought to rest above the hock. The rein is lightly taken up.

The reins are then very cautiously manipulated and gentle little aids given. The pupil usually moves up a pace to the rail, but cannot go forward. It may try to break out, or look over its shoulder, but the reins will check it. I relax and tighten the off-side rein at reasonable intervals, slackening it and even letting it slip to the hock before taking it up again. I will dummy change rein once or twice and finger the reins with the utmost delicacy. Six minutes spent in this way is enough. If I happen to have somebody to help me, and it is sometimes necessary with a nervy animal, then he or she can stand in front of the horse and encourage it, by giving it slices of carrot or pieces of bread. The whole process should be no more difficult than teaching a green horse to give its feet.

The next stage will be a little walk around the yard, in a straight line, but with me taking up the position that I would adopt on the circle in the school. I might even try a circle if things appear to be going well. If all seems to be in order, the next time out will be in the school.

The horse is prepared in the usual fashion, the reins are folded, tied and brought to the withers, and the animal led to the school. I do not have the advantage of an indoor school, but use a lungeing area at one end of a small paddock. This is familiar ground and helps make the pupil confident. It knows what to expect. The circle is relatively small, 30 feet in diameter, the ground is sure and well associated with other lungeing sessions.

The technique is straightforward. The pupil is placed on the circle, made to stand and the reins taken up. What has been done at the hitching rail is repeated, the outside rein being allowed to slide down the crupper and then flipped gently up over the hock. The tutor takes up his position and urges the animal forward. I usually have a dressage whip in my hand in order to give visual indications. My personal technique is to move with the pupil around the circle. I consider this to be a good thing to do. In moving with the horse, I demonstrate that I am working *with* it, which encourages it to go forward by example. My hands will also be softer, the touch finer and in sympathy with the movement. I will be better able to feel my way and to give and take when necessary. And then although I am walking to one side of the pupil, I am really giving it a prenotion of how it will be when I pick up the reins and drive it from behind. That will be the next stage and the step will be half taken by the time that I am ready to take it.

The first session will not be longer than five or six minutes at the most, maybe even less if the pupil appears to be having trouble. The work is strenuous and takes it out of the pupil, so that it is wise not to overtax him. One change of rein may be ventured during that first lesson, and that will most probably be a somewhat messy affair, because the pupil is almost bound to have trouble in understanding what I want to execute. The change of rein is introduced by shortening the outside rein and lengthening the inside one, at the same time putting light pressure on the outside rein as the change-over is being made. When it has been completed, tutor and pupil will make the same number of circuits as were made on the circle before the change took place. That is enough for the start. The pupil is rewarded, praised and either returned to the stable or to the paddock. The whole thing should be done very quietly and without fuss or anxiety. It does not really matter if the work was good or bad, the main thing being that it was done.

It is important to be patient, not to hurry and to remember that the horse is learning and that you are trying to tell it what to do. Do not worry the pupil by asking too much of it too soon. You should not look for any refinement, much less perfection, until you have done a great deal of work and know from experience that the horse is normally capable of delivering better quality.

There is no doubt that the pupil will not live up to your expectations for quite some time. There is no reason to be disappointed by this. The work is strenuous and demands concentration. It is almost certain that the animal will stiffen its back, press down its tail and try to throw up its head. The position of the outside rein will probably make it chop and either start forward, or even mince. Some will overbend and put their noses down between their legs; others will go above the bit when the reins are first attached directly to it. All of this is to be expected and most may be corrected by the tact of the handler.

The real work on the double lunge may begin as soon as these minor problems have been sorted out and the pupil has learned that nothing more is being asked of it than that it should go forward. Sessions should be short and kept so for quite a long time, the number of minutes added being a matter of experience in relation to the particular horse. I start with six minutes maximum and increase the working time session by session.

Being able to see the totality of the pupil is undoubtedly one of the great advantages of double lungeing. You are literally able to observe everything about the horse and what it is doing that demands correction, and you are also able to see what mistakes you may be making yourself which may influence those made by the horse. All mistakes stem from the hands and what they are telling the horse. It is, for example, extremely easy to ask the horse to go forward and, at the same time, put on the brakes, as is often observed in the jumping arena where you can see the mistake before the crash.

Early lessons are therefore not for the pupil alone, unless you are very expert. They should be devoted as much to establishing communication, as to creating a smooth and consistent rhythm, achieved by encouraging the pupil to stretch and carry itself naturally and to find its own balance in this way. The best way of encouraging this, is to allow the pupil to walk on a loose rein until you judge it right to take up the reins a little, in order to achieve the equivalent of the long rein in riding. No attempt should be made to take up the reins until what is wanted has been achieved. When that has come to pass, you may begin to take them up gently and ask for acceptance. The second aim, that of suppleness and relaxation, shows in the whole of the execution of the movement, and almost tells you when to advance step by little step as you go along. This you seek in conjunction with the feel of the mouth; at first the animal tends to lean on the bit and then relax on it as the pupil flexes, until you have 'nothing in the hand'.

You should not attempt to collect the animal at too early a stage, but rather to delay doing so until it moves really well on the taken-up reins and has no fear of balancing and stretching, so that the whole of the top line from poll to crupper shows comfort. I attempt to make the horse move as though it were not attached to me in any way.

Some horses do this very quickly. When they do so, you may then begin to bother about impulsion, for you can have rhythm without impulsion, as, indeed, you may have impulsion without rhythm. The two do not necessarily go hand in hand, however desirable that may be. Impulsion should not be the first aim, not even with a lazy horse. Any animal that you have brought forward to the point of being able to work with it on long reins, should already have the qualities I am speaking about, but there will probably be a slight setback until the pupil adjusts to the new situation and it is wise to allow it to find its balance, as well as to feel comfortable in itself. It is for this reason that you must watch your hands and the effect of them, rather than confuse the pupil. The aim is always the same and should never be lost from sight. You should be thinking of future instant and fine responses to the aids, consistent rhythm, relaxation, acceptance of the bridle – even if the breaking cavesson replaces it for the time being – and ideally, complete communication through what Wynmalen called a 'silken rein'.

There is always the real danger that an inexperienced tutor will go tense and hard on the reins. In other words, he will not give with the hands, but take a relentless grip and continue to punish, because he is not sure that the more or less free animal will not break away from him and so get out of control if he does not keep up the pressure. This is no different to hanging onto the mouth when in the saddle and, naturally, it must be corrected. Such a tutor spoils the mouth for the aids. The reaction is psychological and wrong. The outcome of such cramping on the part of the tutor reflects in the bearing of the horse. It will defend itself against the hand by refusing to relax and usually by overbending, or it may throw up its head and stiffen the neck and back. If the hand is too hard, the pupil may well develop a sort of stiff, chopping gait reminiscent of a badly executed cross between a passage and a piaffe in forward motion. This is as likely to happen in driving as it is in double lungeing.

You may begin to execute various figures when you are pleased with the progress you have made. The pupil moves forward reasonably well at walk and trot, because it is free and relaxed and responds well to the rein aids, changing rein without inhibition when asked to do so.

Once I start work on the school figures, I change my position to behind the horse and begin to drive it. However, the very first thing that I do is to teach it the combined leg and rein aids.

A long touching cane is used when doing this. I use a fibreglass one that is 13 feet long. I need the length, because it must allow me to touch the pupil just behind the girth where the rider's leg would normally do so. I drive the horse forward in a straight line, then press the tip of the cane against the flank, inhale and then apply the rein aid. The pupil will get the hang of this in a few lessons and very soon respond to the 'leg' aid and the following rein aid. What is essential, if you wish the pupil to be very sensitive to the aids when ridden, is the timing and sequence. Both are achieved by the inhalation of your breath as the time pause between the application of the two aids, followed by the *immediate* giving, or relaxation of the rein as soon as the horse shows that it is responding.

You must not hang on to the mouth one fraction of a second longer than absolutely necessary. As soon as the pupil shows that it is obedient to the aid, or even better, as soon as one senses the response coming, even before it actually takes place, you should relax the minimal tension and give praise.

The sequence is, therefore, pressure with the cane on the

left flank behind the saddle girth, an inhalation, application of the rein, followed by praise. The same rules apply in the case of a complete change of hand.

The trainer's footwork should, as in ordinary leading, agree with the horse's. However, the difference is this: while you follow the action of the front feet when leading, you watch the action of the back legs when driving. This keeps you in balance with the movement, which substantially means with the pendulum or balancing motion of the pupil's head. Agreement with this gives you a better rein control while putting you in sympathy with the whole bodily rhythm. In following this rule, you put yourself in a better position to feel your way into the horse, thus making your reactions more sensitive.

This business of feeling one's way into the horse is difficult to explain because it can be neither taught nor learned. If you cannot pick up a horse's vibrations and feel them through your contact with the animal, directly through reins or saddle, then there is no way of learning to do so. But you can attempt it by concentration; by trying fully to understand what the horse is up to at that moment. It is certainly worth a try, if you hope to achieve any harmony at all.

There is little that cannot be taught to a horse on long reins, little that cannot be made and corrected. It does not end with the walk, the trot or turns to right and left and changes of rein. You can go much further with passes and half-passes and work on two tracks, the passage and the piaffe; in fact, everything that a horse may be taught from the saddle. But, one word of warning. There is a strange sense of power when working with an attentive and eager pupil, and with it comes the desire to attempt more and more difficult lessons, to advance the animal too quickly to the status of prodigy. This has to be curbed. If you try to vent your own ambitions on the animal you run the very real danger of overtaxing it and causing a nervous breakdown.

As in all teaching, advancement is stage by slow stage, until the lesson really sticks and the execution becomes almost a second nature when demanded. The same work should not be carried out day after day. You have to vary the diet: leading today, loose schooling tomorrow, lungeing the day after, and long reins the day after that again. This will keep the horse interested and eager to learn, and you can teach it more. You will also ensure that you have a mentally well-balanced animal on your hands.

Nor should you ever overdo the length of time devoted to work on long reins. The work is strenuous, especially if the pupil is concentrating. Remember that the horse is paying attention to you all the time and, in most cases, is actually interested in what you are doing with it. This is something that you may tend to forget. For example, it is quite one thing for a horse to be ridden across country with the unfolding variety of sights and sounds and the freedom of action all there to make life worthwhile and quite another for it to be ridden round and round, say, the inside of a school at walk, trot or canter.

The school figures play as important a role as when the horse is moved under the rider. The serpentine, the figure of eight, the half volte and the volte etc, can be attempted once the tutor becomes handy in the management of reins and horse.

Perhaps the greatest advantage of a young horse that has been so trained, is that it already knows something when it comes under the rider, who can then concentrate on developing and perfecting, rather than having to introduce and teach. After all, every discipline should be the foundation for the next one and should further the individual talent of the pupil. That is surely what it is all about.

Obviously, the more expert horse and tutor become, and the better they work together, the nearer the tutor may work to the pupil, by shortening the rein and coming within 30 inches or so of the quarters. When this is possible, threading the reins through stirrups or rings may be dispensed with and the reins worked directly from hand to mouth, as in riding. But this takes time and you should never expect quick results when working with horses. If you are continuing to teach the leg aids, you should change over from the touching cane to a dressage whip.

I have only touched on long reining as a means of teaching a green horse to react properly to the aids before anybody sits upon its back. That should be sufficient to meet most requirements. More sophisticated work is a matter of personal fascination, but not necessary in trying to achieve your aim: the production of the pleasant riding horse sensitive to the aids.

Teaching the young horse to respond to the rein and leg aids should really be sufficient as a preliminary to preparing it for its first experience in the hands of the rider. It will have learned to understand the aids and to respond to them and will not have to digest the new and simultaneous problems of having to learn the aids, plus the unfamiliar weight of the rider upon its back.

References

1. WYNMALEN, HENRY. *Equitation*, J.A. Allen & Co. Ltd, London, 1971.

CHAPTER 19

Head Control

YOU CANNOT PHYSICALLY CONTROL A HORSE unless you are able to control its head. That is why a head-shy horse is a very difficult one to deal with. A horse that throws up its head, especially a big horse, or one that is not trusting, has the edge on you every time. Experience has taught me this, and it took me two years of patient work to get such a horse right. It was well worth the trouble.

The handler or rider controls the head of the horse, but must also use his own. I always say that a horse is ridden primarily with the head, and the same applies to the daily handling of it. Intellectualism? Maybe, up to a point. I have an American friend who in approaching any problem mutters 'Thinking, thinking, all the time' and how right he is. If you think about the subject at all, the very first thing that you have to do is to think about your own hands, which are so important in the daily life of the horse. It is a prerequisite to good handling to control your hands. You must use them with gentle care and consideration because they will not only control the head, but also every other thing that you do with the animal, from giving it its food to treating injuries. When I speak of gentleness, I am not

talking about approach and spiritual gentleness only; but
gentleness of touch which, however, should not be confused
with firmness and certainty of touch. I have spoken elsewhere of making the horse's head come down to your
hands, and that you should hold them low, at about the
level of the lap because, in so doing, you ultimately come
to control the head which is *given* to you.

I begin head control, as I will now call it, by giving tit-
bits at the end of the day when all is quiet and the horse
and I have a little time to communicate. I make a habit,
whenever I can, of going into the box to have a chat. The
horses love it and come to me, sniff at me, drop their
heads to have them fondled, their cheeks stroked, the polls
scratched behind the ears, their shoulders pinched from
withers to leg. What is five minutes or so per horse per day?
Do I love my charges enough to devote that amount of time
to them? The answer has to be yes. The younger the horse,
the sooner it reacts to this kind of treatment. It is then no
great problem to teach it to accept the headcollar without
fuss.

I have to confess never to unfasten a headcollar. I slip it
over the ears when I am dressing the horse, and in the case
of a horse like Tirade, it is a simple matter because I tell her
'Put it on' and she does so. I stand in front of her, not beside
her, and she stretches out her head to allow the headstrap
to be slipped on over her ears.

The following method can be used to teach a youngster
to accept the headcollar in this way. Hold out your left hand
in the centre of the outstretched headcollar, holding it low;
in the hand, have a piece of carrot or bread to offer the
pupil. The horse's head comes down to take the tit-bit and
the noseband is slipped upwards. Then, while the animal is
enjoying the goodie, say, 'Put it on' and slip the headstrap
over the ears. It takes a little while to do this properly
because the horse does not really understand what you are
doing and may resist. A very young foal has to be forced
at first, and this should be done with great patience, the
little headcollar being put on from beside the animal in the

usual manner. But, as soon as the pupil is fully trusting, you should stand in front of the horse instead of to the side. One must never, never be rough and impatient. Always take time.

I advocate this method of getting the headcollar on the horse because experience has taught me that if I can teach it to be 'dressed' in this way, it will neither walk on my feet, nor give me any trouble. An even greater advantage is that when it comes to making it accept the bridle and bit, half the battle is already won. It is pleasant to be able to stand in the door of the box and have the horse come eagerly to you to have its headcollar put on because it knows that it is going to be taken out. Our pony Leila was difficult for quite a while, but now, as soon as I enter the stable and walk along the short passage, she will watch me intently to see if I reach for the headcollar on its hook. If I do, she will already be standing and waiting with lowered head before I even have time to open the box door.

It is very easy to get a young horse to accept the bit. Once again, I recommend standing in front of it, either at the open door of the box if inside a stable, or at the Dutch door, so that it may lean over in comfort and come down to your hands. Young horses are inquisitive and want to take everything in their mouths, and advantage is taken of this. I take a mild, unjointed bit, preferably made of rubber or vulcanite, smear it with a cut carrot, or apply a little honey, and offer it to the pupil with my thumbs hooked through the rings. As soon as the horse takes it into its mouth, which it will sooner or later, I bring the bit up between the bars, hold onto the side rings of the headcollar with my little fingers, then allow the bit to be savoured until the moment that the horse wishes to reject it. I take care not to hold on a moment longer than the animal will allow, letting the bit slip out of the mouth as soon as I feel the rejection about to take place. I will do this quite a few times before attaching the bit to a bridle. The bridle should be without noseband at first, slipped up over the ears and adjusted *afterwards*. The less fuss the better in putting it on.

You do not want the horse to learn to put up a defence against being bitted and bridled, and it is very easy to do so if you are in any way inept or fumble with the buckles. Once the bit is in the mouth, the horse will adjust it by chewing and one can fix it at leisure, because, curiously enough, even an impatient young animal is quiet enough once the bridle is on. Its thoughts will be with the bit and making it comfortable.

The old dressage horse, Fricka, who used to be with me and whom I used to ride, would start chomping as soon as she saw me approaching her box with the bridle and bit at the ready. I would hold it out to her, she would lower her head and open her mouth to grab at the bit which she instantly began to mouth with a most contented look on her face. That is the ideal situation.

Some care has to be taken, especially when one is teaching acceptance, not to touch the eyes with the bridle cheek straps, and I find it of great importance to insert the bit as quietly and as gently as possible. Unfortunately Tirade never learned to open her mouth in order to accept the bit because her previous rider did not believe in the method and I failed to force the issue. However, she was properly taught by the conventional method and is therefore not difficult to bridle.

While we are on the subject of putting things into horses' mouths, it might not be out of place to say a few words about mouths themselves. A horse's mouth is something rather special and is much more than the orifice through which the food passes before being ground by the teeth.

I have said that head-shyness, which is a man-made fault, requires patience and time to cure, but it can be cured. Not so a horse that has been spoiled in the mouth. A horse that has been made hard-mouthed can never be cured of it and one that has been badly bitted, either with too sharp a bit, or a twisted snaffle or from some other cause, may well become fussy in the mouth. The same may be said of the animal which has to suffer the bit being banged in between its teeth after it has had a cold and unsympathetic bar of metal forced past its lips. A mouth that has been robbed of its sensitivity is irreparable. It is from this knowledge, that I keep on chanting about getting the horse to bring its head down voluntarily.

The horse's mouth is also its hand. The strong rubbery highly flexible upper lip is the finger that does everything. It is equipped by nature with the sense of touch, which is realised through the 'whiskers' or, really, feeler antennae, that are so important to the well-being of the creature. If I had my way, I would impose a fine for the removal of these whiskers in the so-called service of beautification. Without them, the disadvantages are great. The animal cannot feel its way about in the darkness and cannot really sort its food.

Horses touch each other a great deal. They are contact animals *par excellence*, whether they seek contact with humans or with others of their own kind. Therefore, the whiskers, lips and sense of smell are at work all the time. These senses co-ordinate the information that they gather and pass it on to the central nervous system.

Nothing is eaten before it is smelled and touched or even pushed into a new position, if such is possible. The whiskers provide the sensitive sense of feeling, the mobile upper lip tries and arranges, and very often, the mouth will come into play in order to grasp an object already tested.

When something has proved to be of interest, most horses will endeavour to test the texture with their lips. Knowing what an object feels like appears to be every bit as important as knowing what it smells like at close quarters. I say, at close quarters impliedly, because of course the sense of smell which is acute, has long been in operation before whatever it is comes within touching distance. This close combination of scent, feeling of texture, touching and ocular observation, are quite clear when one allows a horse to graze at the end of a leading rein and to cover the terrain as it wishes.

Ordinarily, the majority of horses will take whatever they can into their mouths, be it a rein, the handle of a broom or pitchfork, your own hair if you will let them, the edge of your jacket, or the buttons on your coat, to mention but a few items. For some reason or another, buttons are a great joy to stallions who gladly nip them off if given the chance. But they also seem to fascinate geldings and mares as well, making it wise to wear jackets that close with a zip fastener. They are also very sly when it comes to grabbing things that they should not.

It is unfortunate how many people seem to believe that horses wish to do them harm when they advance upon them with no other desire than to get acquainted. Many a potentially excellent relationship has been nipped in the bud by harsh or hasty rebuttal which the animal will not forget. It has to be remembered that most animals have a certain childlike mentality that puts their approach on a par with that of children. They have no desire to accept the advances of anyone before they have had the chance to make up their minds about them.

Most humans who are unused to dealing with animals have a complex about being bitten by almost everything from a canary to a sheep, and the first question they ask is 'does it bite?' But the only way that a horse knows how to take up close contact is by means of its head which it is careful of and pays you the compliment of offering.

At the same time, it is wrong to try and rush the contact, and the concept that because I love all animals and wish them well – possibly tinged by a shade of wanting to show all present that you are not afraid they will love you automatically, is somewhat Utopian. They won't. I believe in letting a strange horse come to me when it wants to do so.

I wear a special and venerable wreck of a nylon jacket that seems to bear the delicious scent of stallions and mares alike, and appears to make me somewhat acceptable to both. It is the despair of my wife, who would like to sacrifice it to the gods on a pyre, but this is violently resisted. All horses love to rub their faces against it, rest their heads on my shoulder, or blow warm air against my chest if they manage to get their noses inside it. This blowing of warm, used air is very complimentary, and if the soft muzzle comes up against my face and the big nostrils are close to my nose and mouth, I like to return the compliment. This is intimate horse talk that may follow up my slow approach. But when I first meet a horse I like to let him take the initiative and will do no more than stand away from him, the back of a hand towards him, inactive, held low and limp, in order to allow him to decide. It is this very inactivity that the animals understand, and when they do come, it is better to look past them at first.

One must learn to differentiate. The old belief that a horse is full of evil intent if it shows the whites of its eyes or lays back its ears is not correct. Many horses do this. The equine threat posture is unmistakeable. The ears are flattened, the eyes roll, the mouth squares to show teeth, the head extends and is thrust forward on a long neck and sometimes the head is shaken. The whole animal shows tension and there is an ugliness about the posture that ill becomes a horse. It is better to take care. But extreme threat postures are unusual between domestic horses and human beings.

CHAPTER 20

Introduction to the Saddle

ALTHOUGH I HAVE TALKED about the horse being mounted for the first time, in the earlier chapter on standing, and I mentioned that I put an arm across the animal's back in order to accustom it to strangeness there, I will now deal more fully with the method of approach to getting it used to the saddle and what I do in preparation for this important event.

The horse has already been introduced to the headcollar. It has learned about the bridle and bit, now it must become accustomed to the saddle. This is a simple matter and I keep an old saddle especially for this purpose. It will teach the young animal to come to terms with the weight of *anything* on its back. I tether the pupil to the hitching rail, or get an assistant to hold it still by the cheek straps of the headcollar, then gently stroke the back from withers to middle with my hand, pressing down a little. The horse understands this because I have often rested both my arms on its back when grooming. Or, on the days when it is very quiet, I have put an arm over its back as we made our way towards the paddock, leaning heavily for a while. So when the moment comes to slip the saddle gently onto the back and leave it there, the pupil will think little about it and does not even find the strangeness uncomfortable.

The trial saddle has neither girth nor stirrups. This means that it is without any form of physical restriction, or anything that may move or make a strange sound. I take the pupil for a walk about the yard, return to the hitching rail and take the saddle off. I then give it to the pupil to inspect. It is carefully looked over, scented and accepted. After all, the young horse recognises its own scent. This exercise is done at irregular intervals with, maybe, a few days in between. Until one day chosen at random, I slip on the saddle, pass a surcingle over the deepest part of it and secure it. The surcingle should not be pulled too tight. One should be able to place four fingers between it and the animal's belly. The reason I use a surcingle instead of a girth is because it has only one buckle to contend with. While I want the pupil to get used to the idea of something being done up, I do not want to spend a lot of time doing it. Also, when I have finished, it requires only one hand to release the pressure. Once the strap has been tightened, the horse is taken for a short walk during which it is allowed to graze with the saddle on its back. The third time out, the horse is lunged at walk. In this way it learns that there is nothing unpleasant about either the weight or presence of the new experience.

Things begin to move apace after that. Much depends upon the nature of the individual pupil. There is usually no trouble and all becomes a matter of progression. First the girth, then the stirrups are added. Constant practice soon makes the pupil quite familiar with its saddle. Remember that this work is already being done long before the horse will ever come under a rider; while it is far too young to experience any such thing.

Meanwhile, care is taken to make the young horse used to having its back touched and loaded. Light weights are put on the saddle. Fifty pounds of sand in a floppy sack will begin the training and help to harden the back. The saddle, without either stirrups or additional weight, will be up on the back for ordinary walks in hand. Later, when the pupil has been introduced to the lunge and goes properly, the saddle will be worn. If the horse gets hot during lungeing, his back should be allowed to cool before unsaddling him in order to avoid the possibility of soreness. Here the procedure is the same as with the ridden horse.

It is a good idea to prepare the horse by dummy mounting. This is done by placing the hands correctly as if wanting to mount and then applying the appropriate pressure on the saddle. The horse will gradually get used to the left hand above the withers and the right hand along the side of the saddle where it will rest later on with the whip that will prevent him from swinging out his quarters when being mounted. As soon as the pupil learns to stand still and to show no objection to the pull on the saddle, the light weight of a young rider may be placed in the stirrup, and a day or so later, when the horse shows no signs of panic or undue excitement, the young rider may lay his body across the saddle. This should be practised a few times until the rider actually gets up on the horse, there to remain passive, for a minute or so.

It is worth taking time at this stage. The horse will not be ridden for a year or so, and this allows plenty of time. It goes without saying that the rider or whoever gets up, must be careful to lower himself slowly and carefully into the deepest part of the saddle and not to flop down into it. At the same time, if the young horse already knows the bridle and bit, the reins may be taken up and the pupil taught to stand still.

I tried putting up an assistant on Leila. I used a slightly different technique with the pony, the assistant getting up on the bare back, although the animal already knew the saddle, surcingle and girth. We used the technique of a leg up and had no trouble. I also made experiments with mounting blocks and with having the rider stand at a height over the horse. This at first makes the animal rather nervous and demands that you lead and relead it up to the block and person, to overcome its fear.

Anything that will help the pupil's confidence is a good thing. It is good to allow yourself plenty of time in preparing for the future. All work should be done without any sign of nervousness, excitement or fuss. But it should be done deftly and reasonably quickly. Whatever method you use should be discussed with your assistant before getting to work. You have to decide upon the work, day by day, according to the mental condition of the pupil on any particular day. This will vary considerably.

It is good to allow plenty of time when preparing for the future. Remember that a young back, or that of an animal which has been out on grass, is soft and requires special consideration until it hardens up.

Never forget that the lessons being taught are intended to last for life and that they are being taught very early because you are trying to allow plenty of time in order to achieve a certain perfection. For this reason, postponement of work if things are not running smoothly, even if for a few days, is always worthwhile in the long run.

CHAPTER 21

Handling the Feet

IF YOU ARE LUCKY enough to have a horse that has been in your care since its birth, footcare is an easy matter. Foals should have their feet picked up daily even if only for a second or so per foot. When this is done, the foot should be *replaced* gently on the ground, not dropped with a bang. A hand should be run down the leg with the utmost gentleness, the index finger and thumb encircling the pasterns, thereby teaching the young animal that it must allow legs and hooves to be touched at will. The hoof should be picked up and allowed to rest in the cupped hand and not forcibly held by gripping the pastern. It takes very little time, just some practice and patience, to ensure that both vet and farrier will have an easier job when feet or legs require treatment.

Daily inspection of a youngster's legs and hooves should be a routine affair and it is proper to have the foal nearby when this is done to the dam. The foal will learn faster through observation than through anything else. There are those who contend that animals do not learn by watching one another, but this is outside my experience.

As far as the foal is concerned, the time devoted to daily inspection will be increased progressively, and when it allows its feet to be inspected without putting up any resistance, a fairly short, flat piece of metal will be useful. Simply rub this over the little hoof, as a farrier would with a rasp, and tap against the hoof as though one were shoeing.

You should start this training at a young age, the younger the better if you wish the youngster to be well mannered when the farrier visits to work on the dam. Ask him to pick up the hooves of the foal in order to teach the youngster to have its feet lifted by a stranger, and it is wise if he taps and scrapes a bit at the same time.

We all know horses that are difficult to shoe and the struggles that may take place. All this is really not necessary. I expect my horses to be ready to lift a foot when I tell them to do so.

As is so often the case with horses, getting them to cooperate is merely a matter of careful handling, not of shouting or bullying during the early stages when you are trying to teach them what you expect. You must set out to form a good habit based on a reflex. I have seen a young man kicked unconscious by his own mare who refused to have her feet picked up, as well as quite dreadful struggles between spoiled horses and the farrier. Some animals are so difficult in this respect that it is virtually impossible to shoe them. They appear to have what amounts to a real phobia. There are probably many reasons for this kind of behaviour: a bad prick from the hoof pick, actual pain, rough handling, letting the foot hit the ground with an unpleasant bang, bullying by forcing through impatience, injury or simple lack of early education. Who knows?

Some animals lean heavily on the foot that is to be worked on so that no amount of pulling will induce them to lift it or budge it from the ground. A good trick is to tickle them very lightly with the tips of the fingers right down the leg to the fetlock. I have found that even the most obstinate horse will move its foot when asked to in this way.

I owned a mare who gave no trouble when I wanted to

do anything to her forefeet, but who was very difficult as soon as I moved to the back. Since she was generally difficult, I thought that she was merely being obstinate. Then I discovered that doing the hind hooves presented less trouble on dry days, although there was still that reluctance, but the problem was much worse on wet days, or damp ones. This naturally led me to believe that she might be suffering from some pain in the lumbar region or even in the hip joint, because as soon as the hoof was cupped in the hand, she would bear down heavily as though looking for support. After a few experiments to find a comfortable position, I found there was relatively little trouble at all if I drew the hindleg out behind the body in a straight line, or even crossed it slightly over the other back leg, keeping it relatively low.

This experience taught me that an animal which is reluctant to have its feet lifted or, for that matter, to allow you to touch a part of its body, is not necessarily disobliging. In such cases it is better to carry out a careful inspection before deciding that the animal's reaction is caused by illwill. Gently palpate the legs, especially in the region of joints, as well as muscles, both in the legs themselves, and those of the back and along the loins. While doing so, watch for any flinching that might give a clue that something could be wrong. Should such delicate palpation appear to reveal something, then consult the vet.

My Arab mare had a nasty habit of going down on the foreleg when it was raised and of giving a quick backward jerk, thereby neatly removing the hoof from my hand. I believe that she may have been pricked rather sharply with a hoof pick and then developed the habit. I examined her carefully, found nothing and cured her by a sharp slap with the back of my open hand on her shoulder until the day that she decided to stop the nonsense.

Some people like to grip the pastern joint quite firmly when they are picking up a hoof. It is true that this is the least movable of the phalangeal joints, but the coffin joint which is below it in the hoof possesses a great deal of movement which allows the hoof flexibility when being picked up. Many horses, like Tirade, do not like the feel of this and object to it. By holding the hoof in the cupped hand, movement is prevented and, when you have finished the work, the horse will allow you to replace the hoof on the ground.

Teaching an inexperienced two-year-old can be quite a job and I had some trouble with our part-bred Arab pony when she first came to us. Although she had been well handled at her stud farm, she was a little scatty and inclined to frighten easily when faced with things she did not know. Ponies tend to have minds of their own and seem to be a bit on the pig-headed side, so that they need convincing rather than any other kind of treatment until they get to know you really well. But fortunately most of them may be bribed and I did this very readily in order to convince her that it was a profitable thing to give her feet.

I adopted the following method. I would fill a pocket with slices of carrot or cubes of stale bread, then go up to her and give her the hoof pick to inspect. As soon as she had sniffed at it, I would give her a slice of carrot. Thereafter, when I told her to give her hoof, she would get one slice of carrot or a bread cube when she let it be picked up, and another when the hoof was finished. And this for all four hooves. If she pulled away, or kicked out – ponies seem to like to kick out – or swung on her tether, she was instantly rewarded with a sharp slap with the open back of my hand on shoulder or backside, accompanied by an angry 'No'. Then we would start all over again. If she still refused, then she was shown a bread cube or a carrot which she was quite unable to reach and told to give her foot. It nearly always worked. Instead of taking the hoof and working on it, I would put it down gently, give the reward, demand the foot once again and get to work on it. When it was done, she would get the second reward. She was given great praise on the completion of each hoof and, when all were done, an extra reward.

What I have described above is pure reflex conditioning.

It required about two weeks to get this pony to give her feet willingly, and longer before the rewards could be gradually decreased until the moment when one reward at the end of a hoof-picking session was enough. No reward is given today.

However, I make a practice of showing the horses the hoof pick before getting to work, allowing them to sniff at it, just as I offer everything that is used on their bodies during grooming and quartering.

I have already mentioned the mare who had trouble with her back. She is dead and gone now, but her ailment taught me to think a little, as well as to observe all animals that put up any form of resistance. I have observed that most people pick up the hind hooves by lifting the leg so that a right angle is formed by hip joint, hock and cannon, but that the whole leg is drawn away from the barrel, outwards towards the person who is working. This method puts unnecessary tension on the hip joint as well as on the muscles of the area. The whole leg is drawn into a position that is unnatural to the horse. I have already explained what I did in the case of the mare when I pulled the leg back in a fairly straight line in relation to the body, even going to the lengths of crossing the supporting hind leg. This not only allows the horse to keep its balance, but prevents it having to adjust the supporting hind hoof. The advantage is obvious. There is no strain on any of the leg joints, none at all on the hip, and it makes it difficult for the animal to kick out because it must draw back the whole leg in order to do so.

A good farrier will often take the leg between his own legs, supporting it in this way. Without supporting between my legs, I still draw the leg backwards as described and have made it standard practice in my stable.

CHAPTER 22

Traffic-proofing

IN EDUCATING THE HORSE we deliberately equip it with the obedience that is necessary to make it a safe animal, bearing in mind that it is infinitely stronger than we are.

Although our foresight and training may not fully avert accident and death, we can go a long way towards doing so if we understand our horses and learn to bring them gently under control by teaching them to trust us in any situation, especially when we are out with them in traffic and on the public roads.

To assert that this cannot be done would be nonsense. As I have said elsewhere, every police horse is taught to be calm in the face of situations unknown to the average horse.

An article on the high death toll amongst horses and riders on English roads, appearing in the *Irish Equestrian News*[1], gave the alarming figure of 63.6 per cent of the accidents involving horses and traffic, as between horse and rider and vehicle, during the first half of 1980. In other words, horses that were under control. Although the high figure was undoubtedly contributed to by the bad conduct or ignorance of drivers, it is not unthinkable that a fair proportion was also due to improperly trained horses.

I have no hesitation when it comes to repeating what I have said before: horses may be made traffic wise by proper teaching. As in everything else, the devotion of some time and patience is all that is required. It is, of course, useless to begin such a training until the same horse has learned to stand still when told to do so and how to do this has already been discussed.

Although the horses that we keep have learned to behave in the face of traffic, they are given refresher courses from time to time. They are made to stand at the entrance to the drive, facing the oncoming traffic, and are talked to the while. Cars and lorries are moving rather fast here and, because the road curves at this point, they look as if they are coming straight at us. There are no problems when the traffic is coming towards the horses, and even clattering lorries do not frighten them. What may be problematical is the car or lorry that is approaching from the rear and that, despite the construction of the horse's eye, cannot be fully identified. For this reason the horse should also be taught to remain calm by turning its quarters to the direction of the traffic, so that it may experience the sight and sound of something that comes up on it from behind and eventually swooshes past its side.

Horses react differently to traffic sounds and sizes of vehicles, but exposure will eventually teach them that there is little to fear. As has already been recommended, the calm human voice, touch and behaviour will 'infect' the pupil and teach it to learn acceptance.

Teaching should be undertaken at the side of, but as near as possible to, the road, with the tutor standing between the pupil and the road. The best places to teach are at the entrance of a driveway, or within the small turn-in area of a field.

It is wise to teach in-hand during the early stages as one has better control, then, as soon as the nerves are steady after several sessions, from the saddle. I started both of our horses' traffic-proofing when they were very young and had not yet come under the rider, by simply leading them out across the dam that forms our entrance drive and showing them the oncoming traffic. I made a habit of exciting their interest by stretching out my arm in the direction of anything that was coming and calling 'Watch it'. Eventually the animals got the message and began to fidget because they were bored, ignoring the traffic and showing signs of wanting to go home.

I furthered the training by following each horse with a car when it was being hacked home under saddle. This not only gave it cover from other road users, but practice in being passed by them.

Although many drivers behave stupidly in relation to horses, the greatest source of danger is the imponderable, like the wind-blown rolling tin-can, the sheet of paper, or some object that cannot be identified moving behind a hedge. There is very little that one can do about these things as they always represent a hazard even without the additional one of traffic. Nevertheless some training may be under-taken in this direction by creating such 'dangers' through the placing of old newspapers, tin-cans, plastic bags and so on, along a pre-planned route to, say, the paddock, and a rather windy day is a good one to choose for this purpose. The pupil is led on a lunge rein in the safety of an enclosed yard, then there is no danger to anyone if it becomes fright-ened and acts up as a consequence.

References

1. DOUGLAS, AVERIL, 'English Scene', *Irish Equestrian News*, Vol.2, No.2, p.15, March 1981.

Bibliography

BANKO, W. *The Trumpeter Swan*, No. 63, United States Department of the Interior.

BECHER, R., *Erfolg mit Longe, Hilfszügel und Gebib*, Erich Hoffmann Verlag, Heidenheim, 1970.

CANBY, T.Y., *National Geographic Magazine*, Vol. 149, No. 46, June, 1976.

CLOWER, M., *Pacemaker International*, London. June, 1978.

DOUGALL, N., *Stallions*, J.A. Allen & Co. Ltd, London, 1976.

DRÖSCHER, V.B., *Überlebens Formel*, ECON Verlag, Düsseldorf/Wien, 1979.

KLIMKE, DR R., *Cavaletti*, J.A. Allen & Co. Ltd, London, 1969.

KLIMKE, DR R., *Programme Turnier der Sieger*, Verlag Wolfgang Hölker, Münster, 1983.

LAWICK and GOODALL, *Innocent Killers*, Collins, London, 1970.

LONGRIGG, R., *The History of Horse Racing*, Macmillan, London and Stein & Day, New York, 1972.

LORENZ, DR K., *On Aggression*, Bantam Matrix Editions, 1969.

MACSWINEY OF MASHANAGLASS, THE MARQUIS, *Six Came Flying*, Michael Joseph, London, 1971.

MÖRMANN, H. and PLOGER, E., *Buskaschi in Afghanistan*, Verlag C.J. Bucher, Lucerne and Frankfurt, 1978.

MOTTISTONE, THE LORD, *My Horse Warrior*, Hodder & Stoughton, 1934. (Published in Germany as *Mein Pferd Warrior* by Deutsche Verlags-Anstalt GmbH, Stuttgart & Berlin.)

PLAYFAIR, G.L. and HILL, S., *The Cycles of Heaven*, Pan Books, London and Sydney, 1979.

ROSE, M., *Training Your Own Horse*, George Harrap & Co. Ltd, London, 1977.

RIDINGER, J.E., *Schul– und Campagne Pferde* (1760), Die bibliophilen Taschenbücher, Harenberg Kommunikation, Dortmund, 1978.

SCHIELE, E., *The Arab Horse in Europe*, George Harrap & Co. Ltd, London, 1970. (Published in Germany as *Araber in Europa* by BLV Verlagsgesellschaft mbH, 1973.)

SCHIELE, E., *Arabiens Pferde*, BLV Verlagsgesellschaft mbH, 1975.

SMYTHE, R.H. and GOODY, P.C., *The Horse*, J.A. Allen & Co. Ltd, London, 1973.

STERN, H., *Bemrkungen über Pferde*, Kindler Verlag, Munich, 1973.

SUMMERHAYS, R.S., *The Problem Horse*, J.A. Allen & Co. Ltd, London, 1975.

TUKE, D., *Horse by Horse*, J.A. Allen & Co. Ltd, London, 1973.

VAVRA, R., *Pferdestudien*, Co-Libris Verlagsgesellschaft, Munich, 1979.

WYNMALEN, H., *Equitation*, J.A. Allen & Co. Ltd, London, 1971.

WYNMALEN, H., *Horsebreeding and Stud Management*, J.A. Allen & Co. Ltd, London, 1971.

WILLIAMS, D., *Show Jumping*, Pelham Books, London, 1970.

XENOPHON, *Art of Horsemanship*, J. A. Allen & Co. Ltd, London, 1962. (Published in Germany as *Über die Reitkunst* (translation Dr R. Keller) by Erich Hoffmann Verlag, Heidenheim, 1977.)

ZEEB, DR K., *Wildpferde in Dülmen*, 4th edition, Hallwag Verlag, Bern & Stuttgart, 1974.